THE COMPLETE GUIDE TO RUNES

THE
COMPLETE
GUIDE TO
RUNES

*An Essential Reference
for Runelore, Meanings,
Divination, and Magic*

WAYNE BREKKE

ROCKRIDGE
PRESS

This book is dedicated to my parents, Warren and Shila Brekke. Thank you both for always encouraging me to follow my creative path. And to my uncle Ed, who brought his love of books into my life.

CONTENTS

INTRODUCTION

Greetings, dear reader, and welcome to *The Complete Guide to Runes*. It is my honor to bring you this comprehensive treatise about the runes and how these mystical symbols became part of our lives in this modern world.

We all start our runic journey in different ways. Some of us don't even know we've begun the journey until later in life. My own interest in runes started with a Norse mythology class I took in high school. Growing up, I had always loved the fantasy worlds of dwarves, elves, orcs, and Viking-type warriors. I played *Dungeons & Dragons* and discovered the Dwarven runes of Tolkien, not realizing they were based on the Futharks (runic alphabets you'll learn about in this book).

Studying Norse myths in school kindled my interest, but it was much later in life that I discovered my first rune set and book about runes. I immediately felt like I had a connection to runes from a previous life.

After that, I started using the runes in my life and devoured every relevant book I could find and every video I could watch. Encouraged by friends in metaphysical circles, I started casting runes for others and then began teaching clinics on rune use. I taught classes on making runes, rune divination, and using the runes for modern magic. I incorporated runes into other magical works, like the use of crystals and stones in Heathen, Pagan, and other Occult practices. I found they blended quite well in each case.

Runework has been the most rewarding experience of my life and has permeated every aspect of it. I now have a dedicated practice, social media channels, a podcast, a video channel, and now this rune book. It's been a blessing to help people discover what runes are, show how runework can help their lives, and answer questions on runic practice.

I hope this book will become just one in your growing collection of runic reference materials. You'll find a lot of information out there on rune use, some of it confusing, some of it contradictory, and some of it simply untrue. It's up to you to digest the information and take from it what works best for you. It's also common knowledge that runes have been misused over the years by those seeking to twist their meanings for their own nefarious purposes. It's my intention that this book does its part to banish fallacies and bring runes into the modern age for the benefit of humankind. Always remember: Runework should be inclusive, accepting, and based on helping yourself and others.

Using runes can help you experience new facets of life. Runes connect you to nature and the universe. They are the most versatile tools of any divination system, and their use is limited only by your imagination.

Thank you for taking the time to read these words, and I hope this book inspires you to continue your journey with the runes. The world of Norse mythology, the mysteries of runes, and the magic of the cosmos are within your reach. You just need to keep reading.

HOW TO USE THIS BOOK

This book is designed to help you understand the runes and the mythology that brought them to our modern world. It's also meant to inspire you to dig deeper into Norse mythology, and teach you how to use the runes in your daily life.

Use this book as a guide for interpreting the runes, as well as a workbook to foster a solid runic practice. Are you new to the practice of runework? You've reached an ideal starting place! Use this book for study. Mark it up. Break out the highlighter and flag important sections.

The book is divided into three parts:

◆ Part I provides an introduction to the fascinating history and mythology of runes.

◆ Part II contains profiles of each rune so that you can understand their individual meanings and uses in your readings.

◆ Part III shows you how to cast runes, with examples of common rune spreads and a selection of practices for magic, divination, and self-discovery.

It's my goal that by the end of this book, you will have a working knowledge of runes, their history, their use in divination, and how to develop your own runic practices. I also hope that this book will serve as an inclusive guide to runeworking that focuses on the power we all have inside ourselves. You can develop your own runic study program using this book for guidance. Create a book of your own. Journal your experiences and daily rune pulls, and document new information as it comes.

As you make your way through these pages, never forget that working with runes should be a joyful experience. Don't feel bound by any interpretation or practice. Experience the runes as a part of your life, and enjoy the journey.

PART I

An Introduction to Runes and Runelore

The word *rune* translates roughly as "secret" or "mystery," and for good reason. Runes are mysterious symbols that even in today's world are seen in popular culture like movies, TV, video games, and tattoos and are sold in sets in metaphysical stores.

To begin our examination of runes, let's dust off some of the mystery and uncover a bit of the history. It's important for any rune-worker to know something of where these symbols came from and what cultures used them.

This first part of this book covers some of the history of runic writing, describing where these symbols came from and how they were used by the people of the day. You'll learn how runes, and their corresponding deities, are already part of our daily lives, even appearing in familiar places like our names for the days of the week. We'll travel through the various runic Futharks and learn how they were used.

You will also learn about the legends of the various Norse gods as well as the nine worlds of the cosmos. You'll learn about many of the fantastical beings that dwell within the realms of Norse mythology, all to deepen your appreciation and understanding of the cultures and settings from which the runes emerged.

CHAPTER ONE

Entering the World of Runes

Ready to begin? We'll start our journey with an introduction to the various runic alphabets, known as the Futharks. We commonly use the Elder Futhark for divination, but it's important to be familiar with the other Futharks as well, because they play a significant role in the development of runic writing.

Knowing at least a bit of the history of each Futhark system is important when studying the origins of how runes came to be. So we'll discuss the distinctive features of each, why they were developed, and who used them.

This chapter will also inspire your journey of runic discovery by revealing that runes are everywhere once you start noticing them. With that in mind, you'll see how runes can become powerful tools of magic and divination.

The Runic Alphabets

There are many runic alphabets found throughout ancient history, but three remain the most commonly recognized in runework: the Elder Futhark, the Younger Futhark, and the Anglo-Saxon Futhorc. Each of these alphabets are significant in their history and mystery, as they offer important clues to the development of the written language of the Northern people and beyond.

Each also has their place in modern-day runeworking. Elder runes are typically used in divination, and the Younger runes are commonly used as an alphabet for writing. Anglo-Saxon runes are used for both writing and ritual.

During the Viking age, the Younger Futhark became an authentic alphabet, replacing the Elder Futhark as a writing system. But as runes were adapted by Old England and Frisia (located in the Netherlands and northwestern Germany), more symbols were included and transformed once again, into the Anglo-Saxon alphabet.

But long before runes were adapted as an alphabet, the ancient symbols of the Elder Futhark represented elements of nature and cosmic experiences. They were used to tell stories, record lore, and invoke magic. In their journey across time, countries, and cultures, the runes of the Elder Futhark provided a foundation for all the runic alphabets and writing systems to follow.

The Significance of Rune Names: Phonosemantics

An important way to study runes is to discover the connection between their sounds and meaning. This connection helps uncover correspondences the runes have with our daily life and environment. Many rune shapes mimic representations of nature or cosmic elements. Their names and shapes offer clues to their meanings.

For example, Fehu represents the *F* sound and has a general meaning of *cattle*. Livestock represent abundance, wealth, and commerce. Over time, the word "Fehu" evolved into the English word *fee*, relating to the exchange of currency for goods and services.

The rune Ansuz provides an *A* sound and is connected with the god Odin. Ansuz represents knowledge, wisdom, and communication. This word has fittingly evolved into the modern word *answer*.

Some rune names give clues to their meanings readily, such as Hagal (hail), Mannaz (humankind), and Isa (ice). Studying a rune's shape also helps discern its meaning. For example, Algiz can represent the antlers of an elk or the footprint of a raven.

Each rune also has a specific correspondence with the gods, so naturally, the names of the week evolved from them. The god Tyr, represented in Tiwaz, became Tuesday, and the mighty Thor, represented in Thurisaz, became Thursday.

Three Principal Futharks

Among the many runic alphabets and writing systems that evolved over history, three principal futharks remain the most commonly noted today: the Elder Futhark, the Younger Futhark, and the Anglo-Saxon Futhorc.

Each system has a series of rune symbols set in a specific order with its own sound and meaning. Many of the runic symbols overlap, as the futhark system evolved with the expanding language of Scandinavian and Germanic cultures.

The Elder Futhark went out of use around 800 CE as the Norse language expanded, becoming more complex. The Younger Futhark decreased the number of runes and standardized writing. Whereas the Elder Futhark is made up of twenty-four runes, the Younger Futhark has only sixteen.

After the development and common use of the Younger Futhark system expanded, another evolution occurred during Christianization, with more runes and variations added to extend the runic alphabet. This is known as the Anglo-Saxon Futhorc, which was used for writing in Old English and Frisian.

Today, the Elder Futhark is the choice for divination due to its balance of twenty-four runes, though there is no real historical record of how or if they were commonly used for divination or magical purposes.

The Elder Futhark

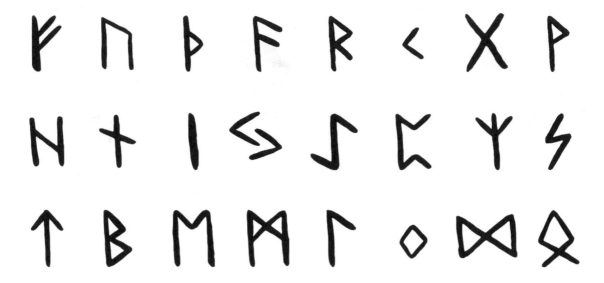

The Elder Futhark is known as the oldest of the futhark systems. Steeped in history and ancient lore, it's the foundation that most other futharks evolved from. One of the oldest confirmed inscriptions that showcased the Elder Futhark in a distinctive order was found on the famous Kylver Stone, which dates to around 400 CE.

As the Greek word *alphabet* comes from the symbols of Alpha and Beta, the word *futhark* is derived from the first six runes: Fehu (F), Uruz (U), Thurisaz (TH), Ansuz (A), Raidho (R), and Kenaz (K), respectively.

The Elder Futhark is organized into three sets of eight runes, known as ætt (or eights). Each ætt corresponds with the Norse god that rules it. The first eight runes are known as Freyr's Ætt, the second are Hagal's Ætt, and lastly, there is Tyr's Ætt.

Each ætt also has an overall theme spread among the runes. For instance, the rune meanings in Freyr's Ætt concern love, abundance, forward movement, joy, and the gathering of knowledge. Hagal's Ætt deals with potential challenges, change, chance, and spiritual connection. Tyr's Ætt focuses on new beginnings, personal growth, partnership, and ancestry. Most rune sets that are sold commercially use the Elder Futhark rune system.

The Younger Futhark

The Younger Futhark is an abbreviated version of the Elder Futhark that was used commonly in Scandinavia after about 700 CE. It contains sixteen runic symbols and has modified phonemes to accommodate what was an expanding and more complex language. Historians note that this transition came quickly, and they are unsure why it evolved into fewer runes to inscribe an even more complex language system.

Whereas the Elder Futhark was used as a symbolic writing system, the Younger Futhark became an authentic alphabet used commonly during the Viking Age. These runes can be found inscribed on items such as coins, stones, weapons, and even graffiti.

The Younger Futhark is organized into four sets of four runes. This system also maintains the Futhark order for the first six runes. The symbols themselves are very similar to the Elder Futhark runes, yet they have expanded pronunciations, depending on how they are used in writing and language. Most runic writing seen in everything from ancient inscriptions to modern video games is commonly based on the Younger Futhark runes.

Typically, most modern rune-workers don't use the Younger Futhark for divination, as it doesn't include some of the most powerful elder runes.

The Anglo-Saxon Futhorc

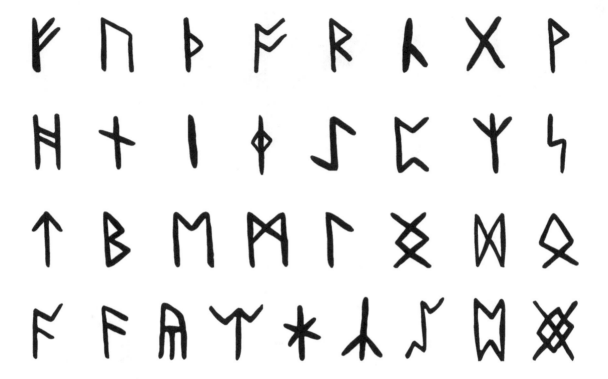

The Anglo-Saxon Futhorc is a modified version of the runes based on the Elder Futhark. As the runes spread and were adapted by the Old English and the Friesians as a writing system, these cultures brought back modified elements of both the Elder and Younger Futhark. In fact, the earliest versions of the Anglo-Saxon runes were almost identical to the Elder Futhark.

These runes are typically organized in four sets of eight and contain many symbols that overlap from previous futhark systems. This system was primarily used from the fifth century CE to the eleventh century CE and has evolved over time to commonly contain thirty-two runes. The runes that made up the Anglo-Saxon Futharks had many changes and additions to accommodate for new phonemes in the language and were adapted for writing and documentation. Across various regions, this system took on many versions, so there is really no one true Anglo-Saxon Futhark system.

The Anglo-Saxon Futhark was primarily used as an alphabet, and there is no record of this system ever being used in rune divination. Regardless, some modern rune-workers do use this system for divination, spellwork, and magical writing, but it is not a common practice.

Other Runic Alphabets

As runic writing in general is thousands of years old, it makes sense that there are several runic alphabets that can be found throughout history. It's important to know a little about how the runic alphabets transformed and evolved over the millennia. This not only helps dispel any misconceptions on rune origins, but also showcases the timelessness of these ancient symbols and how they have continued to weave their way into our daily lives.

The first known runic writing system started with the Alvao writing system, which dates back more than seven thousand years. This system of symbols originated in Portugal and is thought to be the system from which most writing systems developed. From there, we get the Phoenician alphabet (replacing cuneiform writing), which eventually begat the more common Greek and Italic scripts.

You can dive deep into the origins of runic writing and alphabets. Many of these symbols overlapped and were adapted into several systems. Good examples of how the runes crossed continents and cultures include the Paleohispanic writing systems (scripts of the Iberian Peninsula before its conquest by the Roman Empire), which lasted until at least the fifth century CE. Other systems were invented during the second century CE and adopted various runes from other systems, including Iberian, Espanca, and Celtiberian scripts.

Runes Are All Around

As you begin your journey with the runes, you'll start to notice them everywhere. Runes are naturally familiar to us, as they are created with simple shapes that exist in every aspect of our lives. Just take a look outside to notice Fehu in the tree branches, or spy Othala in the patterns of your shower curtain or kitchen tiles. We see them every day in patterns, architecture, and nature.

In Germanic Fatchwerk-style architecture (also known as Tudor or half-timbered), you'll notice a variety of runes, such as Algiz and Tiwaz, as a distinctive wall pattern. Timbers embedded in the plaster form runes used for both protection and decoration.

Runes are all around us, and sometimes these runes are repeatedly brought to our attention for a reason. Many times, we just don't realize it until we start studying the runes and their mysteries. But once your rune journey begins, you'll realize just how prevalent runes are in your reality. When you notice runes in your world, you can tap into their messages, so take note if you keep coming across a particular rune. Journal when runes pop up and you take a second look. They may be there for a purpose.

Reviving Runes

Runes have had a tumultuous past, but as the metaphysical movement of the 1960s and 1970s grew, so did interest in runes. Naturally, because there is little to no historical record of how the runes were used in ancient times for divination magic, practitioners developed systems of their own. This brought to light new ways of using runes for everything from seeking guidance to making magical talismans.

Today, the Elder Futhark has become popular with Wiccan, Pagan, and Heathen practitioners. Rune sets are easy to obtain from local metaphysical stores, and books and videos on the subject of runes and divination are readily available for study.

As the popularity of Vikings and Nordic ways has grown over the past few years, you can find runes in video games, corporate logos, tattoos, movies, and television series. Nordic-themed musical groups create soundtracks that add a fantastical element for those who follow the runes.

Most Viking pop culture is fantasy and not based on historical accuracy (as is rune divination), but we can keep a traditional mindset alive through respectful modern use.

Dispelling misconceptions and negative repurposing of the runes should be a primary focus of modern rune-workers.

The Power of Runes

In their modern use in divination and magic, runes have become a way to tap into the forces that connect us with the spirit realm and the Web of Wyrd (an Anglo-Saxon concept referring to the infinite paths of life itself). The runes as a concept encompass all aspects of life, from birth to death and beyond.

As you attune to the runes, a connection is made, and guidance can be transmitted from them like a radio. Runes derive their power from our own intentions, and we use our intuition to allow them to offer insight. In essence, you are the magic and runes are simply powerful and ancient tools. But divination isn't the only use for runes. Runes can be carried, drawn on the skin, and used in writing spells. They can be made into bindrunes or talismans. Runes are some of the most versatile tools of magic.

◇◇◇◇ *Seeking Guidance*

One of the main reasons for consulting the runes is to seek guidance. When you need personal help in overcoming life's challenges, the runes provide insight. It is said that every human has spirit guides or guardians that watch over us. When asking for guidance from the runes, you can tap into that connection and allow these mystical forces to flow through you. You can also tap into your higher self and subconscious thoughts. The runes offer clues to their guidance, and it's up to you to interpret these clues with an open mind and caring heart. But keep in mind, the runes will always tell you what you need to know, not necessarily what you want to know.

◇◇◇◇ *Gaining Wisdom*

In the myths, Odin obtained the runes from self-sacrifice on the world tree Yggdrasil. Odin was also known for his obsessive quest for wisdom, and the runes were part of that quest. Runes can be one of the most useful tools for acquiring the wisdom needed for navigating chaotic waters. They can reveal hidden truths in a situation, raise warning signs for future endeavors, and provide insight into another person's troubles. They may ask you to take a higher or alternative perspective on a situation. Or they may ask you to learn from mistakes you've made in the past. Remember, wisdom is different from knowledge. Knowledge is power, but it's what you do with that power that shows whether you attained wisdom or not.

◇◇◇◇ *Self-Discovery and Transformation*

Many people turn to runes to help change their lives in positive ways. They look for inspiration and clues within the runes to transform their personal realities. Consulting the runes for self-discovery can reveal aspects that may be hidden due to abuse and negative self-talk. Focus, intention, and connection are the keys to runic transformation of the self.

Daily rune pulls and regular consultation can offer insight to help you reach your personal goals. Talismans and bindrunes (a combination of runes drawn together to form a single symbol known as a sigil) can help bring energy and protection to challenging situations. Transformation can be uncomfortable yet fulfilling. But consulting the runes for every decision will not result in positive change, as you must trust yourself as well. Runes are simply the guides to help you get there.

KEY TAKEAWAYS

From their ancient origins to their place in modern spirituality, runes have provided a way for humans to communicate and connect. In this chapter, we investigated the origins of runes and how they evolved over millennia, changing from a way to communicate with the environment and cosmos to tools for connecting with the spirit realm. Now runes are more prevalent than ever in music, media, and spiritual circles. Practitioners use them for divination to gain insight and wisdom from the spirit realms. But runes have a deep history that started long before they were carved in stone by the German and Scandinavian people. Additionally, keep in mind that:

◆ Ancient writing systems eventually became alphabets during their travels through cultures and continents across millennia.

◆ The three principal futhark systems evolved from other writing systems and alphabets.

◆ The revival of rune use for magic and divination has had a great impact on our modern culture.

◆ Discovering runes in our daily life and environment is all about noticing the patterns in trees, tile, and architecture.

◆ Harnessing the power of runes for self-discovery, guidance, and transformation can foster positive change in our daily lives.

CHAPTER TWO

The History of Runes

Now that you've been introduced to runic alphabets, it's time to go deeper. In this chapter, we'll discuss the history of runic writing systems, as well as a variety of other symbology that influenced the runes as we know them today. Many people think that the runes were first created in the forms that they're seen now and were used to tell fortunes or to cast magical spells in the Viking era. But as you'll see, that wasn't the case.

In the following pages, we'll examine the ancient runic symbols that were first carved on stone more than seven thousand years ago. We'll follow the fascinating history of these symbols across continents as the runes were adapted by various cultures and incorporated into their writing systems. We'll explore how runic writing developed and changed into an alphabet to accommodate an expanding Scandinavian language. I'm also excited to introduce you to the *Poetic Edda* and the *Prose Edda*, two important, centuries-old works that serve as a foundation for Norse study.

Everything in this chapter showcases how runes have endured over the ages. From crude rock carvings to elaborate decorations on jewelry, weapons, and tombs, runes have had an incredible journey.

Unpacking the Historical Origins of Runic Writing

Much like Odin himself, runic symbology wandered through many cultures. Weaving through the millennia, these symbols evolved from simple pictographs into a writing system and then eventually into an alphabet.

Archaeologists and scholars have long debated the origins of runic writing, as most information is lost to time. All that remains are fragments of evidence. What is known about runic writing comes from studying other ancient cultures and their writing systems. The first recognized runic alphabet was the Alvao writing system, which was developed about seven thousand years ago in northern Portugal. This runic-style writing system evolved, moving eastward across the continent. Historians can trace influences through the writing systems of the Phoenician, Greek, Etruscan, and Paleohispanic cultures (up to the fifth century BCE).

Paleohispanic symbols were used by Romans, along with their own writing system, until they evolved into the standard Latin alphabet. Due to strong Roman influence, people eventually stopped using runic symbols as the Latin alphabet was adopted.

During the second century until around the eighth century CE, Germanic people began using runic symbols again, including the use of the Elder Futhark. This eventually led to the development of other runic alphabets.

Runic Artifacts: Fixed and Mobile

Everything we know about runes today comes from ancient artifacts. These artifacts range from monumental standing stones to small personal items found in graves and other archaeological sites. As these artifacts are so ancient, the question of how runes were used for writing, communication, and decoration has been widely debated.

Fixed artifacts include the famous standing stones that showcase runic inscriptions and symbology. These stones marked grave sites and sacred sites, and they tell stories. They were meant to leave a lasting history that preserved clues to an ancient way of life. Mobile artifacts are rare discoveries. These include combs, brooches, weapons, and smaller stones. On these smaller pieces, runes were used mainly as symbolic decoration, charms, or wards.

Today we can use runes in much the same way, but along with making a statement, we can incorporate magical intention. Larger, fixed pieces can be adorned with runes and used as sacred decor. Mobile objects such as pendants, bindrunes, and runestaves can be created and incorporated into our daily lives to invoke intentions, provide protection, and bring abundance.

The Earliest-Known Runic Inscriptions

Over the ages, historians and archaeologists have discovered several surviving artifacts with runic symbology. These tools and standing stones provide clues as to how runes and various futhark systems were used in daily life. One of the most interesting finds was the Vimose comb. Found on the island of Funen in Denmark, it is a personal grooming tool and one of the oldest datable artifacts, from around 160 CE. It contains runes from what we know as the Elder Futhark.

The Kylver Stone (one of the many standing monuments found with carved runes) contains the first example of the Elder Futhark in a specific order. It was dated as being from around 400 CE and discovered in 1903 in Kylver, in the Stanga Parish of Gotland.

The Meldorf Fibula (a brooch for fastening garments) was found and dated to the first half of the first century CE. This spring-case type fibula contains a runic inscription that historians believe is one of the oldest ever discovered.

There are several other surviving standing stones that show excellent examples of the Futhark systems. The Rok Runestone in Sweden from the ninth century uses cipher runes, the Elder Futhark, and the Younger Futhark. A Younger Futhark inscription can also be found on a twelfth-century runestone in Vaksala, Sweden. Other examples include the Gummarp Runestone (dating back to between 500 and 700 CE) and the Bjorketorp Runestone (dating back to the seventh century) from Blekinge, Sweden.

Communicating with the Human World and the Magical World

Though the runes historically were used for communication with other humans, today they are commonly used for tapping into the spirit realms. As each rune has a specific sound and mystical correspondence, we can use them to focus our intentions. This connects us to their aspects, creating a bridge between our realm and the realm of the gods. This bridge between realms can be crossed through rune meditation, singing, chanting, or runic spellwork.

Runes are one of the most versatile magical tools. By knowing the sounds and representations the runes invoke, you can use them in a wide variety of ways. For example, you can use Ansuz to connect with the aspect of Odin, focusing on communication and knowledge goals. Laguz can call upon the aspects of Freya, helping you trust your instincts and go with the flow like water. Thurisaz can give you the power and protection of Thor.

Runes can be used for many magical acts, such as candle rituals, rune grids, bindrunes, and runic scripts. Spells can be written out in the various futhark systems and used to create a closer bond to the gods, spirit, and unseen forces that guide your life.

The Vikings

The word *Viking* brings to mind fantastical imagery of savage barbarians wearing winged helms, plundering and raiding with their shields, axes, and longships. But the Vikings were very different from what we see in modern-day fantasy and TV shows. Vikings didn't have wings or horns on their helmets. They didn't sport runic tattoos or even call themselves Vikings. The word itself was introduced into modern English during the eighteenth century.

Vikings were explorers, traders, warriors, and pirates. "Going Viking" came to mean the act of exploring and exploiting new territories for trade or settlements. It was meant to describe an overseas expedition or raid but is now mistakenly used to describe the people from what we call Scandinavia today (Sweden, Norway, and Denmark) as a whole. But a vast majority of the Norse were common folk who kept their cities and towns thriving.

Viking seafarers brought home goods, treasures, and slaves, but those seafaring warriors and traders also shared many things in their travels, such as language, weapon-making skills, spiritual views, political influence, and agricultural knowledge. Their culture had a deep respect for land and sea, and their knowledge advanced their civilization.

The Germanic Peoples

The Germanic peoples refers to the groups that occupied central Europe and Scandinavia well into the Middle Ages, though scholars debate the use of this term, as it insinuates a common group identity for which there is little evidence. Regardless, much of what we know of these ancient cultures comes from Roman authors who first wrote about the Germanic peoples near the Rhine river in the first century BCE.

Some Roman-era archaeological finds painted a crude picture of the Germanic way of life, and other finds unveiled evidence of a very complex society and economy. Pre-Christian artifacts show that the Germanic-speaking people shared religious views and practices. This became what is known as Germanic paganism, and this belief system varied throughout the Germanic territories. But during the course of Late Antiquity, most of the Germanic peoples and the Anglo-Saxons of Britain converted to Christianity. The Scandinavians and Saxons converted much later.

The Northern peoples had a system of law that used popular assembly to make political decisions, but they also had kings, jarls (chiefs), and war leaders. They were farmers, craftspeople, traders, artists, merchants, and warriors.

The *Poetic Edda*

One of the most important resources of Norse mythology is the *Poetic Edda*, also known as the *Elder Edda*. This collection of thirty-one sagas and stories was derived from an Icelandic medieval manuscript written in Old Norse called the *Codex Regius*. This manuscript is a treasured artifact that was written in the twelfth century. But the sagas themselves are much older than the codex, being told orally over the ages by poets, singers, and storytellers.

The poems of the *Poetic Edda* are a fascinating compilation of Icelandic sagas from various time periods and places. The *Poetic Edda* is somewhat of a "mixtape": its stories don't seem to relate to each other or have a chronological order, but it contains the epic adventures of the gods and heroes of Norse mythology and Germanic heroic legends. Knowing the mythologies and tales of the gods offers an easier grasp of the runes and their meanings.

Norwegian, Danish, and Swedish translations offer those that understand the language an authentic view of the poems, but there are some excellent English translations available, too, among them Jackson Crawford's *The Poetic Edda: Stories of the Norse Gods and Heroes*. Though not a direct translation, this book offers easy-to-understand versions of the poems that tell the stories of the Norse gods and heroes.

The *Prose Edda*

The *Poetic Edda* was written by many authors through various time periods, but the *Prose Edda* (also known as the *Younger Edda*) was compiled by a single person. Snorri Sturluson was an Icelandic Christian monk who created the *Prose Edda* as a manual for writing poetry in a Skaldic verse. He compiled the stories of the gods and heroes from various manuscripts and oral knowledge into poems using this style. This created a flowing, story-like collection of poems that presented a time line from creation to Ragnarök, or the world's final destruction. The *Prose Edda* takes a more subtle approach to the gods, but it still offers an ideal complement to the *Poetic Edda*.

The *Prose Edda* is composed of three parts: the Gylfaginning, Skaldskaparmal, and the Hattatal. The first section, Gylfaginning, deals with the creation myths and eventual end of days of Ragnarök. Skaldskaparmal is set as a conversation between the Jotunn (giant) Aegir and the god Bragi. This discussion weaves Norse mythology and the nature of Skaldic poetic writing together, offering a systematic list of kennings (Old Norse metaphors) for places, people, and poetic language. The last section of the *Prose Edda* is Hattatal, in which Snorri Sturluson offers his own compositions. This section is generally thought to have been created to showcase Skaldic verse and alliteration in poetry as Sturluson saw it.

Understanding Ancient Germanic Beliefs

As a rune-worker, it's important to get familiar with the sources that brought the runes to us. Our modern society is very different from the ancient cultures of the North, and what we know has been pieced together by historians, archaeologists, and scholars. Today, mainstream media is flooded with fantasy depictions of what the ancient Germanic and Scandinavian way of life was like, making it necessary to sift to find the truths about traditions among a myriad of misconceptions. But that is all part of your journey.

It's important to balance knowledge of the old ways with the practice of today. For example, there is little evidence of how runes were used in divination, so most everything results from modern ideas, which is quite okay if you understand how runes were actually used (and misused) throughout the ages.

Concepts like good and evil were not a thing in the Viking age. Rather, order and chaos ruled the moral compass of the time. Today, this concept can offer another viewpoint to further your understanding of life. As you learn the mythologies of the gods and heroes, you can start to understand how these teachings bring deeper meaning to the runes. Many runes are directly associated with the gods, and knowing their backstories can offer insight as to why they appear in a rune reading. For example, runes for wisdom like Ansuz can be associated with Odin, whereas Jera, the harvest rune, can be associated with Freyr. Knowing their stories adds an automatic clarity to the meanings of the runes based on the mythologies.

The "Invention" of the Runes

From an ancient perspective, the runes were symbols akin to our modern alphabet. They were used to communicate ideas, write out magic, and mark sacred sites. They were a part of a culture that didn't see the individual runes as magical objects; rather, they were using them to expand their traditions of language and writing.

So the concept of the "invention of runes" falls to a modern age, linked with Pagan magic and divination. Runes for divination are a writing system mixed with mythological mysteries and magical intention. Runes for divination revolve around the associated meanings of the staves compared to the situation of a querent. We assign meanings to the runes through a combination of studying the ancient resources and tapping into our intuition and knowledge of modern-day rune use.

The Eternal Forces of the Runes, the Worship of Odin

Runestaves may be physical tools, but the rune symbols themselves are of a much greater spiritual significance. Runes represent the forces of nature and the universe. Seeking their wisdom reveals new paths in the Web of Wyrd. The intentions put into the runes call to the primordial energies that shape our existence, offering us insight, answers, and wisdom.

Odin is revered as the Allfather and leader of the gods, but he was also known as a wanderer, constantly searching for opportunities to expand his knowledge and insight. In Norse mythology, Odin attained the knowledge and mysteries of the runes through ritual self-sacrifice. For followers of Odin, his sacrifice is a reminder that an energetic exchange is necessary for spiritual growth. Runes are about gaining wisdom, a pursuit with which Odin was obsessed.

Runes tap into the cosmic forces that make up all existence. The messages received from the runes provide insight as to why challenges present themselves and the importance of overcoming them. It is said that "the road to wisdom is paved with poor decisions." It's this concept that allows us to learn from our own mistakes, appreciate the sacrifices, and find wisdom in those experiences, much like Odin.

KEY TAKEAWAYS

In this chapter, you dove into the history of runic writing and how the runes were used in ancient times by the Germanic and Scandinavian people. To fully embrace the nature of runes as they are used today, you must learn to respect the history and mythologies from which they come. Following are some additional key points to remember:

◆ Runic symbols were first carved thousands of years ago as part of a writing system.

◆ Runes were used on fixed artifacts, like standing stones, as well as on mobile artifacts, like jewelry, weapons, and talismans.

◆ Though runes were used originally for writing and communication, people now use them to connect with the spirit of the Northern people for divination and magic.

◆ Sagas contained in the *Poetic Edda* and *Prose Edda* tell the stories of the gods and heroes of Norse mythology.

◆ Runes today are used differently from how runes were used in ancient times.

CHAPTER THREE

Norse Mythology and Runelore

In this chapter, you'll dive into the exciting world of Norse mythology and what inspires people to work with runes in magic and divination. Norse mythology is packed with fascinating and sometimes horrifying accounts of gods, heroes, giants, dwarves, elves, and people. It paints a picture of how the Scandinavian and Germanic people envisioned the creation and eventual destruction of our world. It shows how they saw the universe in multiple levels of existence.

For many, it is the heroic sagas that trigger a desire to work with the runes. Maybe it's because most of the actual history is shrouded in mystery, or maybe some feel a past-life pull toward learning more about Norse myth and runework. Regardless, runes are a bridge between Norse mythology and modern Norse magic. Each should inspire the other.

This chapter will take you through a world of old, where gods, beasts, and men clashed. You will journey through the myths of the Æsir and Vanir. And you will discover the epic tales that continue to influence modern Pagan and Heathen magical practice.

What Is Norse Mythology?

Powerful gods battling giants, epic adventures, and monstrous beasts fill the world of Norse mythology. Ancient tales passed orally from generation to generation explained the mysteries of life and the universe. These sagas were eventually written down and formed the basis for the religious and spiritual life of the Germanic and Scandinavian people.

The basis for Norse mythology was derived from works like the *Codex Regius* and the *Eddas*. Though these works came after the Christianization of the Germanic and Scandinavian countries, they are founded on oral folklore and tradition that has spanned the ages.

Norse mythology focuses on the fantastic tales of the Norse gods and the nine worlds. These stories chronicle the adventures of mighty heroes, crafty giants, and horrifying beasts. They offer tales of creation and describe the many worlds in the universe. From Odin's quest for knowledge to Loki's mischievous endeavors, these stories and sagas teach about the intricacies of humanity.

Learning the myths of the Norse gods will help build a foundation for runework. As each rune has an associated god, you can decipher meanings based on the stories of that god and what they represent. The more you learn about the mythology, the more colorful your runic experience will be.

The Æsir Gods and Goddesses

The Æsir were one of two clans of the Norse gods, the other being the Vanir. They lived in the realm of Asgard, where they ruled with themes including power, protection, and war. In Norse mythology, the Æsir and Vanir were at war until they were united into one single pantheon.

There are many gods of the Æsir, but we will touch on only a few. Each god has their place as an aspect of our own humanity regarding balance, protection, fertility, power, and love. Each god also has a runic association(s), offering insight to rune meanings. These will be described in later chapters on runic descriptions.

Odin was the one-eyed leader of the gods. He was defined by his obsession with knowledge and wisdom. His wife, Frigg, was the goddess of the sky and represented motherhood, love, and marriage. Thor, Odin's son, was the thunder god and friend to humankind. Baldur was Frigg's son and known as the god of innocence and beauty. Heimdall was the watchman and guardian of the rainbow bridge, and Tyr was a god of war but also a god of justice and balance. Idunn was the goddess of youth and fertility. She gave the gods golden apples that kept them immortal. Loki was technically a Jotun (giant) but was considered part of the Æsir. He was known as a trickster and blood brother to Odin.

The Vanir Gods and Goddesses

There is not much record of the mysterious Vanir. It is noted in the *Eddas* that after the great war with the Æsir, they called a truce, exchanged hostages, and became one with them. They eventually intermarried and ruled as a single pantheon.

Less noted as warriors than the Æsir, the Vanir relied on their magic and heightened abilities to avoid peril. They lived in Vanaheimr, ruling over magic, mysticism, fertility, and abundance. They brought color and life to the gods as well as humankind, using sorcery and magical knowledge to influence others.

Njord was the god of the sea and all its riches. He ruled the wind and brought prosperity to sea-farers and fishermen. He was also the father of Freya and Freyr. He became one of the hostages of the Æsir and went to live with them in Asgard. Freya is the goddess of love, beauty, and sorcery. She was one of the most powerful of the Vanir, and her beauty and skills in magic know no match. Freyr is the brother of Freya and is a god of prosperity, abundance, goodness, and the harvest. He, along with Freya and Njord, went to live with the Æsir after the great war between the gods.

Elves, Giants, Land Spirits, and More

There are many fantastical beings described in Norse myths. The realms of the cosmos were filled with elves, giants, spirits, the fay, trolls, ogres, and other entities. Each of them had an important role in the myths, as well as in the lives of both gods and humans.

The concept of elves is closely associated with the Vanir. It was told that Freya was the queen of the fairies and her brother Freyr was an elf lord who ruled over their home of Alfheim. Dark elves were also known as dwarves, and were master makers. Land spirits and fay folk were creatures of nature that imbued the land with magic.

Jotuns were the giant race that ruled the frozen and bitter cold world of Jotunheim. The giants had many interactions with the gods and were constantly battling them for power. Valkyries were celestial shield maidens who choose worthy souls who fell in battle. They would take half the souls to Valhalla in Asgard and the other to Freya's hall. There were also many beasts included in the myths, such as trolls, ogres, and the famous children of Loki, Fenrir the giant wolf and Jormungandr the world serpent.

Norse Cosmology

The Norse creation story and surrounding cosmology is a fantastical collection of tales derived from the *Poetic Edda* and the *Prose Edda* as well as from various other texts. It focuses on cycles of life and death and creation and destruction. Norse cosmology notes that the worlds of existence weren't created from nothing, but rather from the result of other cosmic forces in action.

These forces are apparent in the creation myth of the Norse with Muspell, a land of fire, converging with Niflheim, a land of frost, resulting in a system of rivers that created a realm of ice in the void of the Ginnungagap. In between these realms was a calm and peaceful land from which emerged a being named Yimr, the ancestor of all giants. He in turn bore children who began the race of Jotun.

From the ice, the primordial cow Audumbla licked free a being named Buri. This started the lineage of the gods, with their grandsons being Odin, Vili, and Ve, who eventually moved against the chaotic giants, killing Yimir and most of the Jotun. They then created the earth, humankind, the stars, the sky, and much more.

Yggdrasil

Yggdrasil is known as the world tree and is said to be the center of all things. It is a great ash tree with branches that extend to the far reaches of the cosmos and roots that go deep into the netherworlds. Its roots drink from the waters of creation at the well of Urd, Mimisbrunnr, and the spring of Hvergelmir. It is this tree where Odin hung himself for nine days, seeking the knowledge of the runes. Yggdrasil holds all of the nine realms in its immeasurable branches and serves as the foundation for the universe as the Norse knew it.

Mythical creatures also dwell within the branches, trunk, and roots of Yggdrasil. Four stags gnaw on its needles (possibly representing the seasons or directions), an unnamed eagle represents wisdom in its branches, and a great dragon named Nidhogg chews at its roots.

Yggdrasil is where the gods would hold court and decide on issues of the cosmos. It is a representation of the center of the universe, as well as the cycle of life. It is the connection to all worlds and can be used to focus intention on reaching out to other realms.

The Nine Worlds

Nine worlds exist within the branches and roots of Yggdrasil. Asgard is the home of the Æsir gods and is ruled by Odin. It contains many halls, including Freya's Sessrumnir and Odin's Valhalla. It was surrounded by a great wall and featured a rainbow bridge to all the other realms, called the Bifrost.

Jotunheim is noted as a harsh land of mountains and snow. Home of the giants, this world has deep forests, treacherous terrain, and dangerous beasts.

Midgard is the world of humankind. Here is where humans, created by Odin and his brothers, farm, build cities, and make war.

Muspelheim is the primordial world of fire. This world was part of the creation myth when it collided with Niflheim. It is the epitome of chaos and home to the giant god Sutr.

Niflheim is a world of fog, ice, and snow. It is home to the spring Hvergelmir and to the great worm Nidhogg.

Vanaheimr is the realm of the Vanir. As the Vanir were gods of magic and nature, it is thought that this was a world of beautiful forests, strange creatures, and wild magic.

Alfheim was a realm of the elves and the fay. It was said that the god Freyr ruled Alfheim as king of the elves.

Nidavellir, also known as Svartalfheim, was the dark underworld of the dwarves, who were master creators and tended to the elements of earth, metal, and stone.

Helheim is the world of the dead, ruled by Hel, the daughter of Loki. This is where the dead went when not taken by other gods. It is depicted as a neutral place rather than a realm of pain and suffering.

The Afterlife: Valhalla, Sussrumnir, and Helheim

There were a few places you could go after death, according to Norse mythology. Which realm you ended up in depended on how you died and what gods took notice. Odin had his great hall, called Valhalla, where warriors who died in battle were brought to feast, drink, and fight without remorse.

Odin had a deal with the goddess Freya, who took half of the warriors who died to her hall, called Sussrumnir, a great hall of honor, feasting, love, and beauty. This split in souls was managed by the Valkyries, Odin's celestial shield maidens. The Valkyries would watch the battlefields as the fighting ensued. They would ride down on their winged horses and choose which of the dead go where, plucking their souls from the field and taking them home.

Most of those who died noble, non-battle-related deaths went to the realm of Helheim. Ruled by Hel, Helheim was a place of peace and relative neutrality, a home for those souls no longer residing among the realms of the other worlds. It was a place that the living could not get to easily, and there was no leaving this realm. The story of Baldur's death states that this is where he went, and none of the gods could bring him back.

Odin's Discovery of the Runes

Odin was obsessed with gaining knowledge and wisdom at any cost. He eagerly sacrificed an eye to drink from the horn of Mimir to gain the wisdom of the cosmos, but that wasn't enough. From his throne in Asgard, Odin watched the three sisters known as the Norns weave the Web of Wyrd, shaping the fates of all others. These sisters were Urd, who ruled the past; Verdandi, who presided over the now; and Skuld, who saw all potential futures. They existed at the roots of the great world tree Yggdrasil, which grows and is fed from the waters of Urd's well.

The Norns wove the Web of Wyrd into strands of fate and carved runes into the trunk of the world tree. These powerful symbols influenced the realities of all of the nine worlds. Odin saw this and longed to gain the knowledge and power the runes provided. But the mysteries of the runes lay deep within the well of Urd, and the sacrifice needed to be great. So, Odin made the perilous journey to the foot of Yggdrasil. Near the roots and over the well of Urd, he hung himself from one of the trees' branches. Looking down into the well of Urd, he pierced his side with his spear, forbidding other gods from assisting him. For nine days, he hung in agony, floating between the worlds of life and death. Peering down into the depths of Urd's well, Odin called to the runes. His suffering was great, but his determination to gain the power of the runes was greater.

After he had spent nine days and nights hanging in pain and on the brink of death, the runes presented themselves to Odin. Floating up from the depths of the well of Urd, strange runic symbols filled his mind with the deep mysteries of the universe. He saw the power they represented and knew that he had achieved what he set out to do. Odin screamed in victory, and when he did, the ropes that bound him snapped, releasing him from his suffering. He fell from the tree, bloodied and broken, ending his torment and quest for the runes.

Odin now had the power of the runes. He saw them in his mind, and the forces of the cosmos filled him with knowledge, wisdom, and power. He became even more wise and learned chants and magic that enabled him to bend the powers of the cosmos to his will. For Odin, the runes were the arcane tools that allowed him to bind his enemies, see the future, influence man, protect the gods, and much more.

This story, though a bit harsh in modern terms, demonstrates that knowledge can be gained through hard work and sacrifice, whereas wisdom can be gained only through lived experience.

Wyrd: The Blank "Rune"

The blank rune included in most commercially sold rune sets is commonly called the Wyrd rune, though it is not an actual rune. It is a modern addition to the runes of the Elder Futhark, and not everyone uses it.

This blank stave was most notably introduced by author Ralph Blum in his series of rune books. His books were met with some controversy regarding the rune meanings, information, and use of the blank rune. Many traditional practitioners use Pertho instead of Wyrd. But using Wyrd can offer a different meaning from Pertho. Wyrd embraces the unknown and signifies that there are things you are meant to experience rather than be told about. It allows one to see a void in a reading that is distinct yet mysterious.

The use of this rune is completely up to you. Experiment with the blank stave. Discover how it directs a reading and signifies the unknowable. It is up to you to decide what works for you and what does not.

For most, Norse mythology is the spark that ignites the desire to follow a runic path. The fantastical tales of the gods and beasts of old entertain and teach us about our own humanity. These stories explain the creation of the cosmos, the entities that live within them, and the worlds where all things reside. This chapter offered a brief introduction to the realm of Norse myth and the epic tales that were passed down through the ages, including those that follow here:

- The nine realms make up the cosmos of Norse myth and the creation story that was the beginning of all things.

- Yggdrasil, the world tree where all the nine worlds reside, is central to the creation story.

- Central to Norse mythology are the gods of the Æsir and Vanir, as well as their roles in the realms they call home.

- The beasts and monsters that populated Yggdrasil and the nine worlds included elves, dwarves, giants, monsters, and mythical beasts.

- Odin gained the knowledge of the runes through self-sacrifice.

- Three cosmic sisters weave the Web of Wyrd, which controls fate.

- The souls of the dead got to the realms of the afterlife according to how they died.

PART II

Reading Runes

One of the most intimidating yet important aspects of runework is learning the meanings of the runes. Each rune describes a part of our cosmos and offers clues to its meaning through its sound and shape.

In part two of the book, we will explore the three sets of eight runes of the Elder Futhark, known as ætts. Each is associated with a corresponding Norse god and has a central theme. Don't feel like you need to know all the meanings before using runes. It will be an ongoing journey. Trust your intuition and devote the time in study, practice, and meditation needed to access deeper insights.

The descriptions include both forward and reversed meanings. Some choose not to use reversed meanings, and some suggest beginners focus on the forward aspects first. That said, being able to interpret reversed runes can lead to more impactful readings. It also takes time and practice to understand the runes in positions such as past, present, and future.

Casting and laying out runes may at first seem like an act of randomness. Divination taps into internal forces of the rune-worker as well as external cosmic ones, so have confidence in yourself and know you are not alone when consulting the runes.

CHAPTER FOUR

The First Ætt

The first ætt (eight) of the Elder Futhark is typically associated with the god Freyr, the Æsir god of peace, virility, good harvests, sunshine, and fair weather. It is also associated with his twin sister, Freya, the goddess of fertility, love, sex, war, and beauty.

Each of the runes in this ætt offer connections for experiencing and interacting with both humans and the gods. These runes have a positive energy tied to commerce, community, health, love, protection, and the pursuit of wisdom. They are excellent for magic and rituals that are related to these areas.

In magical use, these are the go-to runes for promoting wealth, health, and protection. They are ideal for use in talismans, bindrunes, and candle rituals. The traits associated with Freyr and Freya can help you enhance your sex life, bring abundance to your bank account, help you heal illness, and keep you safe from danger.

Freyr's Ætt also features the runes of Fehu, Uruz, Thurisaz, Ansuz, Raidho, and Kenaz. The first letter of each is put together as the acronym Futhark, with the two remaining runes being Gifu and Wunjo.

Fehu

PRONUNCIATION: FAY-hoo

ALSO KNOWN AS: Fé and Feoh

SOUND: *f* as in "father"

TRANSLATION: cattle, fee, and wealth

KEYWORDS: abundance, cattle, cycle of transaction, financial wisdom, generosity, and wealth

In ancient times, the more cattle a family had, the wealthier they were. They had enough to sustain them and others in their community. Fehu can be thought of as a personification of abundance. This abundance is enough to foster generosity, and in turn, the betterment of yourself and others, and this cycle of wealth is what powers Fehu. It's not a mentality of hoarding, but of transaction in a way that benefits people and their communities.

Whether in the past, present, or future positions, Fehu's appearance in a reading indicates that finances are the focus. Perhaps a financial boon or opportunities to make more money are on the horizon. It may be that you are in an exciting transition period, looking at new opportunities or collaborations.

Fehu asks you to evaluate your current financial situation. Is it unbalanced or is it flush? Have there been opportunities for wealth-building lately? Did you come upon good fortune or are you experiencing financial freedom?

Either way, your wealth and finances will soon be offering you an experience that will help you grow. Keep an eye out for chance encounters, dreams, and messages from spirit that will help guide you. Trust your intuition and approach money in a loving and generous way.

If Fehu appears reversed, a period of financial struggle or the loss of something valuable, such as money, possessions, or even self-esteem, may be on the horizon. Reversed, Fehu suggests looking ahead and planning for any contingency. Changes might come up that will hinder you if you are not prepared, so get practical and creative with finances.

CORRESPONDENCES

GODS: Freya, Freyr

STONES/CRYSTALS: aventurine, cinnabar, emerald, jade, moss agate, and pyrite

HERBS: basil, clove, ginger, High John the Conqueror, mint, and nettle

COLORS: gold, green, light red, and yellow

TAROT: The Tower

PRACTICAL USES

- Use Fehu with intention rituals of abundance for yourself, others, or in a place of work.

- Carry a Fehu symbol in your wallet to draw wealth to it.

- Use the rune Fehu in grids alongside corresponding crystals and stones.

- Create a bindrune of Fehu and other runes to encourage abundance.

- Carve Fehu into food to keep a full pantry even when times are hard.

- Write Fehu on your skin before a work shift to encourage tips and sales.

Uruz

PRONUNCIATION: OO-rooz

ALSO KNOWN AS: Ur, Urox, and Urus

SOUND: *u* as in "usurp"

TRANSLATION: aurochs (wild ox)

KEYWORDS: forward movement, healing, health, motivation, power, and protection

Uruz represents the massive, prehistoric aurochs, a great ox with powerful horns and hooves. Its large stature and connection with the environment is associated with vitality and healing energy. A powerful healer, this rune offers motivation to get through tough times or help the body and mind overcome injury or trauma.

Uruz in a reading may indicate that you are currently experiencing a vital time in your life. This could be in areas of health, creativity, and motivation. Forward movement with a drive toward success is in focus in your life if this rune is cast in the present. If you are struggling with issues related to motivation or health, Uruz urges you to focus on your ability to overcome them. Let the runes tell you what challenges or inspirations may be affecting you in this area.

If Uruz is reversed in a reading, poor health or lack of motivation is the primary focus. It also may indicate that health problems, such as physical illness and recovery, or mental issues, such as loneliness, anxiety, or lethargy, may be inhibiting progress. Depression may be a result of stagnated energy, and creativity may be at an all-time low.

Now is the time to focus on personal health. The surrounding runes may indicate what path is best. Whether related to mental or physical health, it is imperative to address issues in a way that promotes healing and vitality.

CORRESPONDENCES

GOD: Vanir

STONES/CRYSTALS: black tourmaline, blue calcite, blue lace agate, clear quartz, dendrite, elite shungite, golden healer quartz, green calcite, onyx, and selenite

HERBS: camphor, coriander, devil's shoestring, juniper, mugwort, rue, sage, Saint-John's-wort, spearmint, thistle, and thyme

COLORS: black, clear/white, dark green, light blue, moss green, and red

TAROT: The High Priestess

PRACTICAL USES

- Use Uruz with intention rituals, grids, and spells for healing, gaining vitality, and maintaining motivation.

- Trace the rune Uruz on water glasses or bottles, speaking intentions of health and vitality to the water before drinking.

- Employ Uruz in bindrunes to bring vitality, good health, protection, and forward movement.

Thurisaz

PRONUNCIATION: THOOR-ee-sahz

ALSO KNOWN AS: Thorn and Thurs

SOUND: *th* as in "throw"

TRANSLATION: Thorn, Thor, Giant, or Giant Slayer

KEYWORDS: destruction, power, protection, and strength

Thurisaz is a powerful rune. It represents both protection and an aggressive attitude toward challenges. It can also represent Thor's hammer Mjolnir, also known as the "Giant Slayer." Thor was Odin's son and the god of the common man, of the farmers, bakers, and blacksmiths. He represented the determination and hardiness of everyday people. Regarding protection, the look of the Thurisaz rune can represent the thorn on a stem or a rose.

If Thurisaz is cast in a reading, you may be facing a phase of power and motivation. There may be large obstacles at hand, but you are facing them head-on. Hold fast, knowing that even if you can't see the end result, you must forge ahead.

In mythology, Thor charged ahead to face the giants, no matter how big they were. You can equate "giants" to obstacles that impede your daily life or path. Trust that you have the tools available to overcome these obstacles.

Thurisaz is also a protective rune, and this protection is available to you. Take the time to evaluate your situation to ensure there is nothing working against you in unseen ways. Do not charge into battle without putting your armor on first. Cleanse, ground, and recharge yourself each day so that you have the vitality and clarity to face the challenges ahead.

In a reversed position, Thurisaz may indicate that you are currently facing challenges that are taking their toll on you. Maybe there are feelings of vulnerability and you are feeling over-whelmed. You may feel as if there are no tools or resources at your disposal and that you are exposed to whatever life throws at you. Fear and uncertainty may be influencing your decisions, or you may not be taking the time to think things out properly and are feeling the results of that.

Surrounding runes will show what other aspects are currently influencing your situation. These may indicate the challenges you are facing or where your focus should be at this time. They may also provide clues as to why you are feeling unprotected or vulnerable.

Now may not be the time for harsh actions, but rather a period of examination of the situation. Make sure you stay cleansed, grounded, protected, and recharged on a daily basis.

CORRESPONDENCES

GOD: Thor

STONES/CRYSTALS: black tourmaline, bumblebee jasper, carnelian, clear quartz, fire agate, Libyan desert glass, moldavite, obsidian, onyx, sapphire, Shiva Lingam, shungite, sunstone, and yellow calcite

HERBS: carnation, cinnamon, cinquefoil, devil's shoe-string, dragon's blood, houseleek, mulberry, saffron, Saint-John's-wort, and thistle

COLORS: amber, black, and bright red

TAROT: The Emperor

PRACTICAL USES

- Drawing Thurisaz on the skin stimulates boldness, courage, defense, power at work or at home, and protection.

- Use this rune in grids with corresponding crystals to activate power and protection.

- Employ Thurisaz in bindrunes to overcome challenges and release blockages.

- Make a protective sigil using Thurisaz to keep a car, home, or sacred place safe.

Ansuz

PRONUNCIATION: AHN-sooz

ALSO KNOWN AS: Aza and Oss

SOUND: *a* as in "autumn"

TRANSLATION: answer or mouth

KEYWORDS: air, breath, communication, Loki, knowledge, mentorship, Odin, and wisdom

Ansuz is the rune of communication in all its forms. It is Odin's rune and a rune of wisdom and the attainment of knowledge. Wisdom is usually acquired through experience and learning from the world around you. Communication is key to understanding attained knowledge, and wisdom refers to how you use that knowledge.

Gaining insight on a situation usually requires communication, which could include noticing what is not being said. Odin had many experiences in his quest to obtain knowledge and wisdom. Learning from mentors, elders, masters, and teachers is a core aspect of Ansuz.

Ansuz is also a rune connected to Loki, a god associated with mischief and trickery. Reversed, aspects of Loki appear with Ansuz, as miscommunication and a lack of knowledge lead to unwise decisions. Sometimes, others lie to us or attempt to manipulate us with their words, and these forms of nefarious communication should be noticed.

Communication in this context can take many forms. It could represent chanting, conversation, guidance, instruction, meditation, poetry, prayer, selling, service, singing, and speech. Each offers a way to obtain knowledge through an exchange and acceptance of information.

In a reading, Ansuz shows that communication is a focal point in your life at the moment. You may be gaining knowledge somehow, such as from a mentor or friend. Or maybe you have recently had to speak publicly and/or are working on something that you will need to present to others in a clear and concise way. You may be receiving knowledge from an instructor, therapist, or elder.

Whatever is happening in your life, this exchange of information is key to where you are going. Take note of where this information is coming from and who you are communicating with, and find the hidden lessons. Trust your instincts and enjoy the benefits of patience.

In the reversed position, Ansuz indicates that words are not currently in your favor, and that you may be experiencing a lack of communication. Possibly, there is a rift in a relationship due to miscommunication or deceit. You may be in need of wisdom and patience, as you may feel neither. You might be wondering what to believe, whom to trust, or where you can find answers.

The Loki aspect could be affecting your life as well, with misinformation leading you astray or confusion occurring due to secrets and lies. It could also indicate that this is a time for you to be more clever and cunning. Use your talents to plan and counterplan.

You may be in a transitional period. Take every opportunity to gain wisdom and knowledge. Don't be afraid to reevaluate and take a step back to see things from a higher perspective.

CORRESPONDENCES

GODS: Loki and Odin

STONES/CRYSTALS: blue apatite, elite shungite, emerald, and labradorite

HERBS: bodhi, iris, peach, sage, and sunflower

COLORS: black, dark blue, and silver

TAROT: Death

PRACTICAL USES

- Trace the symbol or name of Ansuz on your body with oil or ink before speaking in public.

- Carry the rune Ansuz for support during difficult conversations.

- Use Ansuz in bindrunes for success in anything that has to do with connecting with others.

- Call upon Ansuz in ritual for wisdom and growth.

- Create a bindrune using Ansuz before going into any speaking situation.

- Draw Ansuz on yourself to better communicate your truth.

Raidho

PRONUNCIATION: Rah-EED-oh

ALSO KNOWN AS: Raeith, Raida, and Raitho

SOUND: *r* as in "ride"

TRANSLATION: journey, riding, wagon, and wheel

KEYWORDS: forward movement, journey, mobility, and travel

Raidho is associated with forward movement in various forms. Associated with a wagon or chariot, it invokes energies of travel, transport, and journeying. This travel can be physical or spiritual, depending on the situation. Raidho can indicate a life or spiritual transformation, vacation, movement in a career, or transition from one home to another. This rune typically indicates a pleasant journey with opportunities for growth, joy, and knowledge.

Raidho in regards to forward movement could refer to selling a home or car or relocating. Activities that foster forward movement in your life and your path are all aspects of Raidho. One can imagine the Norse going "Viking" and traveling to raid or explore new lands. You may not be pillaging exactly, but rather plundering through a new path in life, exploring new destinations and experiences. As on any journey, you must be prepared. Travel takes patience and preparation. This rune can also offer protection on journeys, keeping travelers and wanderers safe and on course to their destinations.

Raidho in a reading indicates that you are currently on a journey, whether physically or spiritually. Regardless, you are on a path of discovery and growth. You are moving from one place to another, whether in business or relationships. You are protected on this journey. You have prepared well and are ready to face the challenges ahead with confidence and ease.

Runes surrounding Raidho may indicate other aspects that are affecting this journey. They may offer insights into goals and aspects of your life that are destinations or currently influencing your experiences.

Reversed, Raidho may indicate that you are experiencing a lack of forward movement. This can be physical, spiritual, or mental. You may be feeling stagnation in your homelife or career. Creativity and motivation may be low. Alternatively, it also points to issues impeding travel.

Look to surrounding runes to discover aspects that are hindering forward movement. Having Raidho in this position is a welcome indicator that your current lack of movement needs addressing.

CORRESPONDENCES

GODS: Ing, Nerthus, and Thor

STONES/CRYSTALS: ametrine, aventurine, bumblebee jasper, chrysoprase, lepidolite, and turquoise

HERBS: holly, mugwort, and oak

COLORS: blue and bright red

TAROT: The Hierophant

PRACTICAL USES

◆ Use the Raidho rune with corresponding stones to create a rune grid for empowerment and forward movement.

◆ Create a bindrune focusing on Raidho for safe journeying.

◆ Write, engrave, or use oil or saliva to inscribe Raidho on luggage when traveling to get to your intended destination safely.

◆ Use Raidho in manifestation rituals and ceremonies to promote forward movement.

◆ Burn Raidho on walking sticks and canes to promote stability and ease of movement in daily life.

Kenaz

PRONUNCIATION: KAY-nahz

ALSO KNOWN AS: Chaon, Kaun, and Ken

SOUND: *k* as in "kind"

TRANSLATION: knowing, torch, or ulcer

KEYWORDS: courage, creativity, discovery, hope, illumination, motivation, and torchlight

Kenaz is the rune of the creative passion that drives us forward. It is the torch that we carry in our lives that leads us through darker times. Kenaz can represent the hope we keep when facing difficulty, both outside and within. It imbues the spirit with a "can-do" attitude.

I have found that Kenaz can be used as a focus for motivation, determination, and dedication. In readings, it can represent hope, creative breakthroughs, or a willingness to do what it takes to accomplish your goals.

Imagine being an explorer, deep in a cave system. Your torch lights the way forward, allowing you to discover new details with every step. The torch offers hope to keep going even if you can't see where you started or where you may end up. If the torch drops and goes out, you might stop in your tracks and experience sudden hopelessness.

In the forward position, Kenaz can represent a time of creative passion, hope, or breakthrough in some area of life. It points to a fire burning within that keeps you motivated and willing to continue on the journey. It may also be that you feel like you are carrying a torch of hope for yourself or others. Cultivate a passionate attitude for your endeavors and moving forward.

In some cases, Kenaz can indicate that you are taking the lead in some project or supporting others by keeping the path in sight. You may be searching for something or partaking in studies that fuel your passions. Whatever it is, know that you have the torch light with you and the determination to see it through.

Reversed, Kenaz indicates that you may feel like you are drifting through life with no direction or motivation. When this is the case, look at this time as an opportunity for direction-setting and growth. What is the course correction you need? This rune in this position may confirm your current feelings and situation, but it also shows that if you take action toward finding that hope and light, you will gain direction and inspiration. Light your inner torch and find ways to see into the darkness. It may be difficult and it may be scary, but Kenaz is telling you that the torch of hope is accessible to you.

CORRESPONDENCES

GODS: dwarves and Freya

STONES/CRYSTALS: aventurine, bloodstone, bumblebee jasper, and celestite

HERB: cowslip

COLOR: light red

TAROT: The Chariot

PRACTICAL USES

◆ Carry Kenaz as a creative talisman that offers hope and inspiration.

◆ Use Kenaz as the focus of a bindrune for inspiration, hope, and strength to overcome obstacles.

◆ Set up a rune grid with Kenaz as the focus while working on art or creative projects.

◆ Give the rune Kenaz to another person who needs a light in their darkness.

Gifu

PRONUNCIATION: GEH-fu

ALSO KNOWN AS: Gefu, Gebo, Giba

SOUND: *g* as in "gift"

TRANSLATION: gift

KEYWORDS: equal exchange, generosity, gift, giving, offering, and receiving

Gifu is the "gift" rune—the gift of the gods and the rune of exchange. It is also the rune of generosity without expectations. The symbol of Gifu is that of an X, much like a ribbon on a wrapped package. This makes it a nice reminder of the rune's meaning. This is also the first rune in this order to not have a reversed position. It is a rune of balance, tempered with happiness and appreciation.

Gifu embodies the act of giving without expectations. It is about generosity from the heart and the acceptance of gifts from others. These gifts can be anything, including physical presents, unexpected money, a boost in your career, or an act of kindness when truly needed.

Gifu can also mean the act of mutual exchange, a win-win attitude, and a pay-it-forward spirit. It can also mean knowledge, which is considered a gift from the gods. This could be advice, a mentor, or just a needed heads-up. But Gifu is also about mutual exchange and the ability to truly accept gifts—to feel gratitude without guilt, shame, or unworthiness.

In a reading, this rune does not have a reversed meaning, but it can still point out issues. For example, someone could give you a compliment and mean it, but you may feel unworthy of the praise, and negative thoughts may rip away any pleasure you may have otherwise felt. Don't keep yourself from receiving. Accept the gift and pass it on.

Gifu may be saying you are giving too much. You may be extending yourself too far without receiving anything in return. This may be taxing on your body, mind, and soul. In this case, look to receive more to recharge your spirit even if it's from yourself. Gift yourself the rest you need so you can continue to do what you do.

In matters of love, look for balance. A relationship should be a win-win situation, where both parties give and receive willingly and honestly. Love is said to be a "two-way street," and if you look at the rune, there are two roads present.

In a reading, Gifu may want you to recognize the gifts you currently have and appreciate them for what they are and what they have taught you. In most cases, Gifu will indicate a time of appreciation and joy. Thoughtfulness and gratitude are important now, and the lessons you are learning are important for your own development.

CORRESPONDENCES

GODS: Freya and Odin

STONES/CRYSTALS: amazonite, blue lace agate, lapis lazuli, opal, and rose quartz

HERB: heartsease

COLOR: deep blue

CHAKRAS: heart, third eye, and throat

TAROT: The Lovers

PRACTICAL USES

- The symbol for hugs and kisses is XOXO, which includes the symbol of Gifu, to show love and compassion.

- Write Gifu on a bay leaf and burn it in ritual to bring the spirit of exchange and gratitude to life.

- To engage the spirit of Gifu, write a small X when signing a card for a special occasion.

- Create a rune grid with Gifu as the focus rune to encourage the spirit of exchange and gifts from the gods.

Wunjo

PRONUNCIATION: WOON-yo

ALSO KNOWN AS: Huun, Winja, and Wunio

SOUND: *w* as in "wonderful"

TRANSLATION: joy

KEYWORDS: accomplishment, bliss, joy, peace, success, and victory

Wunjo represents joy, victory, and satisfaction. Imagine a victory banner raised in the name of happiness and success. When Wunjo appears, it means that it is a time for joy and happiness. In relationships, it points to good fortune and success.

It is a rune that calls upon the energies of positivity and productivity. It represents a completion of something that has forwarded your growth. Wunjo asks you to look back and appreciate the journey that got you to where you are now. Look at the lessons learned and allow yourself the pleasure of feeling happy and proud of your accomplishments. Wunjo is also associated with Odin and his powerful magic, which can manifest wishes and desires. The satisfying energy from this rune comes from the completion of a goal or desire and the wisdom gained from the experience.

Being a rune associated with Odin, it shows us that victory truly comes from appreciating the journey as well as the accomplishment, no matter how difficult the challenges were. Without challenges, there would be no growth. Without recognizing what we learned along the way, we are bound to repeat the same mistakes and travel the same path.

In a reading, Wunjo may indicate that it is time to look at what you have achieved and appreciate the journey up to now. Celebrate everything you have overcome and learned, and enjoy the feelings of satisfaction. If you are currently working on something, Wunjo appears to let you know you have the power, motivation, and will to fulfill your desire.

Reversed, Wunjo may indicate a current feeling of dissatisfaction and defeat. Surrounding runes and consultation will help pinpoint the issue, but regardless, challenges abound. This could be in any area of life, from career to relationships. It's all about your mental state and looking into your ego, attitude, and the situation, along with mental and spiritual health issues that need to be addressed. Consider how you are approaching the issues that are appearing in your life. Realize when your ego and passion may be getting in the way of learning and growth. Keep pushing to find ways out of your negative situations with new strategies, and know that your guides are there to help you.

CORRESPONDENCES

GODS: elves and Freyr

STONES/CRYSTALS: calcite (blue, green, orange, Caribbean, and honey), carnelian, chrysoprase, clear quartz, diamond, and sunstone

HERBS: apple blossom and flax

COLORS: purple, red, and yellow

CHAKRAS: crown, sacral, and solar plexus

TAROT: Strength

PRACTICAL USES

◆ Picture Wunjo as your personal victory flag, and carry the rune with you to remind you that you are fighting for your own happiness.

◆ Write Wunjo on you as a reminder throughout the day to keep up the good fight for success and foster a happy, blissful attitude in yourself.

◆ Use Wunjo in a runestave or rune grid with other runes that promote the manifestation of your desires.

◆ Make intentions with Wunjo for happy relationships and teamwork and to raise the vibrations in your environment.

◆ Use Wunjo in a candle ritual along with other runes to manifest victory and happiness.

KEY TAKEAWAYS

Freyr's Ætt begins the Elder Futhark and focuses on the forward movement of life. From gaining wealth and abundance to finding joy in the little things, Freyr's Ætt signifies the energy needed to overcome challenges. The healing energies of Uruz, protection of Thurisaz, and connection of Ansuz allow you the tools for getting ahead in life. Where Raidho offers the vehicle of transportation, Kenaz brings the light and motivation to get to your destination. Exchange through Gifu results in the joy of Wunjo, completing this set of eight runes with the inspiration and validity we are all searching for. Additionally, remember:

◆ The first letters in the first six runes of this ætt create the acronym of FUTHARK.

◆ Freyr's Ætt focuses on moving forward and bringing abundance into your life.

◆ Combinations of runes in this set, such as Uruz and Thurisaz, offer healing energy and protection from negativity.

◆ Loki, Odin, and Thor are represented in Thurisaz and Ansuz. Using these runes in ritual can call in the traits they represent.

◆ Freyr's Ætt calls to us to remain hopeful, continue moving forward, and not to take the little joys in life for granted.

CHAPTER FIVE

The Second Ætt

Hagal's Ætt is the second set of eight runes in the Elder Futhark. This set has a primary focus of overcoming challenges, connection with the higher self, protection, power, renewal, change, and, finally, victory. These aspects drive us forward and teach us how to navigate the challenges the universe throws at us to better our lives.

Many of these runes have no reversed meaning, but each must be considered with a balanced outlook. Where Hagal offers a short-term pain for a long-term gain, Isa asks us to go within to find our truth. Yet in the middle we have Jera, a harvest, and after the harvest, a renewal. This ætt also connects us with the Web of Wyrd, using Pertho as an aspect of randomness that offers opportunity and luck when all else fails.

Algiz asks us to connect with our higher selves, to experience life in all its glory without fear, and to enjoy the good times and learn from the mistakes. The ætt ends with Sowilo, the sun, serving as a reminder that the sun always rises the next day, even if it's cloudy. Life goes on, and every day means a new chance to become a better person. Look to Hagal's Ætt when the focus is self-care. When life is at its most challenging, this is where you will find the power and the wisdom to see the day through.

Hagalaz

PRONUNCIATION: HA-ga-lahz

ALSO KNOWN AS: Haal, Hagal, Hagalas, and Hagl

SOUND: *h* as in "hail"

TRANSLATION: hail

KEYWORDS: challenges, delay, disruption, hail, renewal, and unexpected change

In its simplest form, Hagalaz represents hail, or the energy that hail brings. It is not a rune to be afraid of; on the contrary, it offers challenges meant to bring us insight and growth. Remember, hail comes on quickly and doesn't last for very long. When it melts, its water flows into the earth, providing nourishment for plants to grow.

Hagalaz is here to help you understand that sometimes short-term pain yields long-term gain. These challenges are not meant to break you or keep you stagnant. They are designed to stretch your critical-thinking skills, test your knowledge, and strengthen your ability to face issues rather than run from them.

This rune signifies obstacles that are out of your control, challenging your need to be in control and pushing you to deal with these situations free from that feeling. Hagalaz is neither good nor bad. It is a teacher, a guide, and an awakening. In a reading, Hagalaz could indicate that challenges and obstacles feel like they are hindering your life path. Each is irritating but each can be overcome.

Hagalaz can show that you are experiencing a time of growth. The universe is throwing challenges at you, but these are specific to your path and how you should proceed. They may not be pleasant, but they are there for a purpose. Challenges are happening not to beat you down, but to show you things you need to be able to overcome to become your future, best self.

Current challenges may also be showing you parts of your life that need adjusting. Consider any triggers and anxiety that you may be imposing on yourself, reactivity that may be leading to issues, and decisions based on emotion that can be better made with a different attitude and higher perspective.

CORRESPONDENCES

GODS: Heimdall, Hel, Urd, and Ymir

STONES/CRYSTALS: black tourmaline, jet, obsidian, and onyx

HERB: lily of the valley

COLORS: light blue and white

TAROT: The World

PRACTICAL USES

◆ Use Hagalaz in runestaves or rituals to invoke quick changes in your life.

◆ Call on Hagalaz for luck that causes a quick change in your situation.

◆ Invoke Hagalaz for help in changing negative habits or addictions. This will bring the challenges needed to overcome them.

◆ Use Hagalaz in rituals to signify a sacrifice for further growth. Offer it with a tribute.

Nauthiz

PRONUNCIATION: NAW-theez

ALSO KNOWN AS: Nauth, Nied, and Nod

SOUND: *n* as in "need"

TRANSLATION: need fire

KEYWORDS: basic human needs, constraint, necessity, need, and restriction

Nauthiz represents the needed fire. The rune itself looks like two logs laid atop each other, ready to be lit. This could be a hearth or a large bonfire. Fire brought warmth and comfort to homes and villages in the ancient North. Consider how a small campfire on a cold night can be an important part of survival. It is a rune about basic human needs, such as warmth, shelter, food, companionship, love (both for self and others), family, joy, and balance. Nauthiz has no reversed interpretation.

Nauthiz is not about things that are wanted for comfort, but rather for basic survival. It can be easy to get caught up in things you think you need but don't impact your ability to survive, and Nauthiz asks you to use wisdom in all matters of budget and finance. It challenges you to make the sacrifices needed now to provide a strong foundation for life so that you can enjoy abundance and comfort in the future.

When Nauthiz appears in a rune cast, it can be asking you to examine your situation and options. If you have limited options, it is telling you to create more. Open yourself up to new opportunities, as Nauthiz burns for your growth.

Nauthiz in the present shows that some basic human needs are currently in focus in your life. You may be working to survive, and Nauthiz shows that you are trying to build a fire to warm you through your physical or metaphorical winter.

What is holding you back? Is it anxiety, fear, lack of confidence, or self-loathing? Are you experiencing a lack of drive, motivation, or depression? Find those blockers and throw them in the fire. Keep the fire burning, for if you do, you will survive the chilling frost of life.

CORRESPONDENCES

GODS: The Norns—Skuld, Urd, and Verdandi

STONES/CRYSTALS: black tourmaline, carnelian, and lapis lazuli

HERB: bistort

COLORS: black and blue

TAROT: The Devil

PRACTICAL USES

- Use Nauthiz in a runestave and burn it in a fire to find new opportunities.

- Employ Nauthiz in a bindrune for help overcoming obstacles and to make sure your basic needs are met.

- Call on Nauthiz for the protection of your home and family.

- Carve "Nauthiz" in a candle during rituals to keep your basic needs met.

Isa

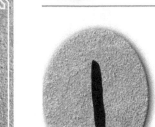

PRONUNCIATION: EYE-sa

ALSO KNOWN AS: Eis and Iss

SOUND: *i* as in "ice"

TRANSLATION: ice

KEYWORDS: calm, clarity, frozen, halting, ice, icicle, inner work, self-care, and self-examination

Isa represents ice. It's about a halting of things and a focus inward. Picture yourself in the middle of an icicle. You are surrounded by a protective shield of ice. You have no distractions. You have nothing but yourself and the truth on which to focus. It is a place of peace and wisdom. Isa appears when you need to look deep inside, without the influences of the outside reality to distract you.

In a reading, this rune could mean that Isa wants you to halt your daily routines to focus on yourself. It could be an indication of the need to stop working so hard and take time to relax. It could indicate that it is time to focus on what you really want in life.

Regard Isa as a blessing, a rune that wants you to take time for you, whether you want to or not. It tells you that your higher self is calling with messages for growth. No matter where it lands, consider Isa a sign that your intuition knows better than your conscious self and that you should strengthen that and not fear the time you take for yourself.

There is no reverse meaning for Isa, much like Nauthiz and Hagal. It is a rune of contemplation for growth. Eliminate distractions to better hear your higher self and tap into your intuition. Truths, solutions, inspirations, realizations, and answers wait for you here. What you do with this information is on you.

In the present, Isa means that a a pause, or halting, is necessary to tap into the answers within, which you need to overcome current obstacles. It doesn't mean just taking time to meditate and "go within," but rather to listen to yourself for needed information. Isa wants you to look around you to see why this halting is needed. What are the truths you won't admit to yourself?

Self-care is required, so find time to relax and enjoy something that is outside of your normal routine. Even if things seem fine, make sure they stay that way by observing the meaning of Isa when it appears. Keep yourself recharged, balanced, and focused on your end goals.

CORRESPONDENCES

GODS: Rime and Thursur

STONES/CRYSTALS: blue apatite, cat's eye, celestite, and tourmaline

HERBS: blackthorn, henbane, and rosemary

COLORS: black, light blue, and white

TAROT: The Hermit

PRACTICAL USES

- Focus on Isa as a safe place for meditation, as if you were in an icicle, free of any distractions.

- Use Isa in a bindrune to facilitate self-evaluation and growth.

- Draw Isa on a candle and burn it while meditating to stop unwanted habits or gain insight from the divine.

- Call upon the energy of Isa to amplify clarity and focus.

Jera

PRONUNCIATION: YEE-ra

ALSO KNOWN AS: Ar, Gaar, Jer, and Jeran

SOUND: *y* as in "year"

TRANSLATION: year

KEYWORDS: accomplishment, annual cycle or seasonal cycle fertility, fruition, growth, harvest, partnership, reaping the rewards of hard work, and year

Jera is known as a rune of the harvest—a symbol of a completion of a cycle or reaping of a job well done. Looking at this rune, you can see the plow and shears, the symbols of the harvest.

It is a balanced rune and can also indicate a partnership or team effort, as any successful harvest takes contributions from more than a single individual. A harvest is best cultivated when all parties involved are appreciated, such as the sun and the rain, the horses that pull the plow, and the folks that helped plant the seeds. Even when we think we are the only one responsible for our success, it is always good to remember we didn't get there alone.

Jera signifies success that is earned and not dropped onto your lap. It is a success that is borne from a time of planning, tending, fertilizing, watering, and then, finally, cultivating. Year after year, season after season, farmers go through this process. They work with what the weather gives them, they find solutions to droughts, they make sure the land is fertile and do what it takes to keep it that way, and they make sure their equipment is maintained.

Jera is also a rune of cycles and seasons. For centuries, humans have based their lives and civilizations on the cycles of the seasons. Cycles make us grow, expand, and adapt. In this way, it's good to note when Jera is asking us to look at our own cycles. This wisdom can be used individually, much like a farmer uses the knowledge of the seasons and climate to plan their harvests. If we can realize when we are going through a cycle, whether in passion, productivity, creativity, depression, or stagnation, we can prepare for or end the cycles.

In a reading, Jera may be asking you to have a plan for the future to ensure you have a bountiful harvest. Give yourself credit for the work you have done when the time comes. Remember that even though you have harvested a crop, the work doesn't stop there. Prepare for the next season to create sustainability in your life. This will allow you to always look forward to a period of satisfaction and accomplishment. There is no reverse position for Jera.

CORRESPONDENCES

GODS: Bragi, Freya, Freyr, and Thor

STONES/CRYSTALS: bumblebee jasper, carnelian, moss agate, pyrite, and tree agate

HERB: rosemary

COLORS: green and light blue

TAROT: The Fool

PRACTICAL USES

◆ Inscribe Jera on a candle and dress it with cinquefoil and other herbs for prosperity and a bountiful outcome.

◆ Use Jera during feasts to honor the gods for the gifts of food and drink.

◆ Invoke Jera when working on a common goal or project with a team or partner.

◆ Use Jera in fertility rituals to encourage pregnancy.

◆ Focus on Jera when participating in any creative endeavors, such as music, art, or theater productions.

◆ Access Jera's energies when taking classes for higher education or learning for a career.

Eihwaz

PRONUNCIATION: EYE-wahz

ALSO KNOWN AS: Eoh, Iwaz, and Yr

SOUND: *i* as in "eye"

TRANSLATION: yew tree

KEYWORDS: letting go, life cycle, protection, regeneration, regrowth, spiritual growth, transformation, world tree, and yew tree

Simply stated, Eihwaz is a symbol of the cycle of life and death, renewal, and regeneration. It is about letting go of things that don't serve you to make room for new growth. It is yet another rune that has no reverse position.

Eihwaz also represents the yew tree and the world tree, Yggdrasil, which extends into all worlds and the universe. In ancient times, the wood from the yew tree was used for making bows, as it was strong yet flexible. Eihwaz asks us to be the same when facing obstacles. Stand strong, yet be flexible enough not to break. The yew tree contains toxins used to make poison. Yet as an evergreen, it symbolizes life. Here is another metaphor for the balance this rune offers. If there are toxins in your life, get rid of them to make room for new, healthy personal growth. The yew can live for thousands of years, and when it begins to die, a new sapling sprouts from the decaying trunk, keeping the life cycle of the tree going through death and rebirth.

When this rune appears in a rune cast, examine your situation and yourself. Look for things that are holding you back from attaining what you want. Seek out the sources of resistance you are experiencing and attitudes in yourself that hinder your growth.

In the present, Eihwaz can signify that you are currently going through a cycle of change. Things are being let go of that no longer serve you, and you are up for the challenge. New growth is happening, and you should recognize the lessons presenting themselves, as they will help you greatly in the future.

This may not be a comfortable experience, but it is one that will be satisfying upon its conclusion. You have the strength and drive to see this cycle through. Your goals are set to be realized, and though it may take patience and perseverance, the outcome will be well worth the time and effort. Take time to appreciate the benefit of your situation and where it may lead you. Remember the lessons learned and what you did that was beneficial to your growth and well-being.

CORRESPONDENCES

GODS: Idun, Odin, and Ullr

STONES/CRYSTALS: smoky quartz and topaz

HERB: mandrake

COLOR: dark blue

CHAKRAS: heart, root, and solar plexus

TAROT: The Hanged Man

PRACTICAL USES

- Use Eihwaz in meditation, focusing on grounding, seeing truth, letting go, and opening up to new growth.

- Carry Eihwaz with you to focus your energy on the cycle of life, particularly on completions and new opportunities.

- Use Eihwaz to develop your psychic abilities, offer yourself protection, recall past lives and lessons, and banish negative energies.

- Carve Eihwaz with other runes to create a bindrune for continued growth, power, and renewal.

- Use Eihwaz alongside Uruz for healing and transition.

Pertho

PRONUNCIATION: PER-tho

ALSO KNOWN AS: Pedro, Perth, Perthro, and Perthu

SOUND: *p* as in "play"

TRANSLATION: dice cup

KEYWORDS: chance, decisions, dice cup, luck, mystery, opportunities, secrets, universal magic, and unknowns

Pertho is one of the most mysterious runes. Its mystery derives from the various meanings of chance, secrecy, and the unknown. Pertho is also used in place of Wyrd for those who choose not to use the blank stave in readings. But it can have a much different meaning when used with Wyrd.

It is often known as the dice cup, as it has the look of a cup or bag that gaming dice are held in and poured out of. Dice are tools of randomness, offering the opportunity to take chances and allow the Web of Wyrd to decide fate.

If you play dice games, you know the excitement of the mystery of randomness. You may even understand when to roll and when to pass. You may have amazing luck at first, only to end the game with a loss due to a few unfortunate dice rolls. Such losses hold lessons in strategy and how to dodge and weave out of unpleasant situations. It can teach you about patience, humility, teamwork, and positive competitiveness.

Pertho indicates that unknown forces are at play. These could be positive or negative depending on the situation, but know that this rune is about working with the unknown. It is about examining your strategy by looking at the options the universe presents you. Take into consideration your experience thus far and use that wisdom to make your choices moving forward.

The question is: If Pertho is the dice cup, then do you even have dice to roll? If forward, Pertho says yes. If reversed, Pertho could indicate that you don't have the dice to roll with. Depending on the surrounding runes, Pertho may be suggesting that you don't take chances with your present situation. Important decisions should not be left to chance.

Expecting the unexpected and preparing to work with whatever happens is a key focus point when dealing with Pertho energies.

CORRESPONDENCES

GODS: The Norns

STONES/CRYSTALS: amethyst, aquamarine, aventurine, blue apatite, and pyrite

HERBS: aconite, basil, and devil's shoestring

COLOR: dark blue

TAROT: The Wheel of Fortune

PRACTICAL USES

- Use Pertho in rituals to help in decision-making when many options are on the table.

- Inscribe Pertho on a dice cup to summon luck in a game or gamble.

- Meditate with Pertho for spiritual guidance, healing, and clear thought.

- Wear Pertho as an amulet during childbirth.

Algiz

PRONUNCIATION: AL-geez

ALSO KNOWN AS: Elhaz and Eolh

SOUND: z as in "zebra"

TRANSLATION: elk

KEYWORDS: antlers, defense, divine connection, elk, peace, protection, and sedge plant

Algiz is a powerful rune of protection. It represents the great elk and its protective antlers. It is also said that Algiz represents the sedge plant, a thorny plant that elk love to eat. The shape of this rune looks a lot like a human being with its hands to the sky, seeking a divine connection for guidance and wisdom. Algiz also symbolizes protection for a group, and homes in Germany, France, and Scandinavia often have this rune built into the structure. This design is known as Fachwerk.

As a protective rune, Algiz offers the energies of confidence and steadfastness. Like a shield, it can be used to ward off negative influences and anger and keep you from harm. Use Algiz with Raidho when traveling for a safe and protected journey. Licking a finger and drawing it on your forehead or carrying a talisman with Algiz can provide protection on the go.

Algiz provides cosmic connection. It represents the ties human beings have with the cosmos and the forces that guide daily life. It's ideal for connecting with your spirit guides or those helping you from beyond the veil. Algiz can be the rainbow bridge that connects you to divine energy and facilitates a higher perspective to help you access needed protection, strength, and determination.

In a reading, Algiz in the forward position shows that protection is at hand—that a connection between you and your guides or gods is active. Listen to their messages and seek further wisdom, knowing you have a steadfast handle on your situation. It may indicate that challenges are ahead from which you will need protection. Look for signs or messages that can help you.

If Algiz appears reversed in a reading, it can point to feelings of vulnerability, fear, and disconnection. It may feel as if challenges are met with no protection, and their impact feels greater than necessary. Algiz may be asking you to connect with higher powers for guidance. Protection and wisdom are needed to move forward.

Meditating and standing in the position of Algiz can offer a rewarding spiritual experience. Its shape is so common that it offers a familiar power whenever it is invoked. Just looking outside, you can notice Algiz in the trees and in nature, reminding you that protection is all around you, if you only challenge yourself to find it.

CORRESPONDENCES

GODS: Heimdall and Valkyrjur

STONES/CRYSTALS: amethyst, angelite, celestite, labradorite, and tektite

HERBS: angelica, sedge, and yew

COLORS: blue and gold

TAROT: The Moon

PRACTICAL USES

- Lick your finger and draw Algiz on your forehead for a blessing of protection.

- Create a talisman or carry the Algiz rune to keep you safe from harm when traveling.

- Hang a sigil of Algiz above the door of your home or incorporate it into the design to keep the house protected from outside forces.

- Make a hand signal that can be used to ward off negative energies by holding up the pinky, index finger, and thumb. This is also the sign for "I love you" in American Sign Language.

Sowilo

PRONUNCIATION: So-WEE-lo

ALSO KNOWN AS: Sigel or Sol

SOUND: s as in "sun"

TRANSLATION: sun

KEYWORDS: energy, light, power, sun, and sunlight

Sowilo is the rune of the sun. As the last of the runes in Hagal's Ætt, it balances the frigid aspects of Hagal and Isa with its radiating warmth. This rune has no reversed position, and it can indicate when power is needed, being provided, or is being wasted, depending on surrounding runes.

Imagine a perfectly sunny day at the perfect temperature. The energy of Sowilo is like the warmth of the sun on your face. No matter what your situation may be, the energy of Sowilo finds its way inside, even if it's cold outside, like sunlight shining through a window on a chilly day.

The sun is a symbol of eternal power and life-giving energy. The Norse goddess Sunna is represented by Sowilo and offers warm, feminine energies that foster growth and forward movement. It is about the connection to the higher self. Sowilo is also associated with the Norse god Baldur and is a guide to help us do the right thing when striving for a positive outcome.

This rune can indicate that a victory is at hand and that joy can be taken from this win. Its shape is similar to a lightning bolt, signifying a strike of power that can connect you with cosmic forces. Like Thor calling down thunderous bolts of energy, Sowilo can initiate an eruption of power. If a boost of energy is needed for a specific project or issue, Sowilo can bring epiphanies to alter outcomes in your favor.

As it has no reverse position, Sowilo can also be seen as an indication of where extra energy is needed. Depending on the surrounding runes, it can show what aspects of your life need a boost or where your focus should be placed. When Sowilo appears, know that you have the full power of the sun behind you. Use it now to achieve your victory, as the sun eventually sets and rises anew.

CORRESPONDENCES

GODS: Baldur, Sol, and Sunna

STONES/CRYSTALS: gold, ouro verde quartz, ruby, and sunstone

HERBS: mistletoe and Saint-John's-wort

COLORS: silver, white, and yellow

TAROT: The Sun

PRACTICAL USES

◆ Carry the rune Sowilo with you to draw confidence and motivation.

◆ Create a sigil using Sowilo to keep with you for power and over-coming obstacles in work and family matters.

◆ Use Sowilo with Raidho when traveling to protect yourself from harm and foster a pleasant journey.

◆ Combine the energies of Sowilo and Uruz for powerful healing.

◆ Draw the rune's symbol or name on your skin or create a bin-drune to combat illness.

KEY TAKEAWAYS

Hagal's Ætt is a set of runes that highlights the fact that overcoming obstacles is necessary to move forward in life. These runes also focus on aspects of your higher self and how you can break down barriers within to find the light. They point out that most of life's problems can be navigated by examining your own energies and how imbalances can create chaos. Hagal's Ætt has many nonreversible runes and runes of ice and impediment. But in the end, this ætt provides the warmth of the sun, serving as a reminder of how connection leads to wisdom. Other key takeaways follow:

◆ These are runes of challenges, like Hagalaz, which means "hail," letting you know that short-term pain can lead to greater, long-term gain. They are meant to show you wisdom and connection with your higher self.

◆ Runes like Nauthiz and Isa ask you to look inward for what you truly need.

◆ Many of these runes can be used to bring power, change, and victory into your life.

◆ Look to Hagal's Ætt for aspects of knowledge, luck, power, protection, and renewal.

CHAPTER SIX

The Third Ætt

The last eight runes in the Elder Futhark are known as Tyr's Ætt. Tyr is the god of honor, justice, legalities, and war. He represents things that require determination, patience, resolve, and sacrifice. Tyr stands for fairness and doing what is right, even at the sacrifice of yourself. These eight runes follow that theme while incorporating aspects of inspiration, working with others, going with the flow, and maintaining power when darkness threatens. In contrast to the challenges of Hagal's Ætt, this set of runes melts the pain and recognizes the gain.

New beginnings abound in this set, with Berkana being a "mother rune" and Ingwaz a seed just starting to grow. Laguz is the water that feeds us, and Dagaz is the dawn that starts the new day. Othala is the last of the runes related to aspects of the home, protection, and ancestral roots.

Tyr's Ætt has many runes from which you can pull power, inspiration, and guidance. These runes focus on the beauty of others, the shine of the human spirit, and the eloquence of the spoken word as passed down through generations.

Tiwaz

PRONUNCIATION: TEE-waz

ALSO KNOWN AS: Tew, Tiw, and Tyr

SOUND: *t* as in "Tuesday"

TRANSLATION: Tyr

KEYWORDS: duty, honor, justice, legalities, male energy, responsibility, and war

Tiwaz is represented through the Norse god Tyr. He is the god of justice, legalities, and war. He sacrificed his hand to the great wolf Fenrir to maintain the scales of balance and justice. Tiwaz also represents success, victory, and power. This rune has a male energy and can often represent a man in a relationship. It is protective, with a shape that is similar to an arrow. You can use Tiwaz when facing physical or intellectual challenges. It was said that Tyr was a leader of the gods and was a master of the strategies of war. You can call on these strategies when you need a specific plan of attack for a situation or obstacle.

Tiwaz is also a rune of balance. If your issues result from an imbalance in your life, Tiwaz asks you to examine the parts of yourself that are out of balance, from your chakras to your homelife. Without balance, you can fall just trying to cross the street, but with balance, much like a tightrope walker, you can cross the Grand Canyon step by step without falling into the void.

Honor, integrity, self-sacrifice, and strength are all aspects of Tiwaz. This rune reminds us that all things worth having are worth working and fighting for. What needs to be done must come at your own expense, and Tiwaz appears to say that valiant efforts will be rewarded.

If Tiwaz presents itself in a reversed position, it could indicate that there is an imbalance in your life. This could present as a feeling that things don't seem fair, or there could be a legal matter that needs your attention. It can also indicate issues with a man in a relationship, a loss of male energy, or a loss of a recent legal battle.

Tiwaz is a powerful and complex rune. It can offer protection and motivation. It can also bring justice to unfair situations. Call upon Tiwaz to restore balance, bring peace, or add intelligent strategy to any situation.

CORRESPONDENCES

GODS: Mani and Tyr

STONES/CRYSTALS: amethyst, fluorite, garnet, halite, and malachite

HERB: sage

COLORS: bright red and orange

TAROT: Justice

PRACTICAL USES

◆ Carry the rune Tiwaz with you when seeking balance in your life.

◆ Make a talisman of Tiwaz when going into any legal setting or courtroom.

◆ Write "Tiwaz" on items used for personal protection to keep you safe from harm.

◆ Invoke Tyr through the use of Tiwaz in runic crystal grids using the stones associated with this god and Tiwaz as the center focus.

◆ Write "Tiwaz" on your person to bring protection and strategic energies to your day.

Berkana

PRONUNCIATION: BER-kahn-ah

ALSO KNOWN AS: Beorc, Berkano, Bjorken, and Brica

SOUND: *b* as in "birth"

TRANSLATION: birch tree

KEYWORDS: birch tree, birth, fertility, healing, mother, new beginnings, and new ideas

Berkana signifies new beginnings, new ideas, and rebirth. Its shape is a reminder of the breasts and belly of a pregnant mother, and it is tied to the Birch Goddess Bercha or Bertha. Berkana represents fertility, both in humans and in crops and livestock. It evokes the fertility of the land and all things within it.

When Berkana presents itself, it is a good sign that new things are on the horizon. These things can take time, patience, and care to come to fruition, but they are in the works. The aspect of "new" is commonly scary to some, so Berkana shows that there is nothing to be afraid of and that your ideas are valid and worth seeing through.

Berkana can also point to unexpected new changes. Sometimes, a pregnancy can happen unexpectedly, and so can situations and ideas. New beginnings may not have been on your mind, but when your higher self is ready, Berkana confirms that the time is right to start something new. In the context of rebirth, it can mean that this is a time to actively look for a new path or direction. Call on Berkana when looking for a new job, lover, or artistic inspiration.

Berkana is also a healing rune. Like a mother, it represents the loving care you can give to yourself and others. It offers a very feminine energy and is ideal for use by women for recovery from illness or injury. Birch oil and tea made from birch leaves provide a calming and healing sensation, and the mushrooms that grow on the birch tree's trunk are amazing antioxidants.

If Berkana appears reversed in a reading, it can indicate a period of stagnation. Now may not be a time for starting new things. Focus on existing priorities before starting something new. It could also represent a time of loss or struggle to find a new path after a traumatizing incident.

CORRESPONDENCES

GODS: Bercha, Bertha, Frigg, Hel, and Nerthus

STONES/CRYSTALS: aventurine, moonstone, pink tourmaline, and rose quartz

HERBS: birch and lady's mantle

COLORS: dark green, pink, and white

TAROT: The Empress

PRACTICAL USES

- Draw the rune Berkana on the belly for healing and to promote conception.

- Use Berkana in a bindrune with Uruz for recovery from illness or injury, especially for women.

- Invoke Berkana when looking for new ideas, projects, or creative inspiration.

- Carry Berkana with you to job interviews and while looking for new career paths.

- Use Berkana in rune-consecration rituals and ceremonies to tap into her feminine, creative energy.

- Use Berkana around the new year to call in rebirth and new beginnings by adding the symbol to food or incorporating it into any new-year ceremony.

Ehwaz

PRONUNCIATION: EH-waz

ALSO KNOWN AS: Eh, Exauz, and Eya

SOUND: e as in "empty"

TRANSLATION: horse

KEYWORDS: cooperation, horse, loyalty, movement, partnership, and sudden changes

Ehwaz is a rune of the horse. It represents close partnerships, loyalty, mutual respect, and trust. The symbol itself can be seen as a horse from the side, with the saddle in the middle. It can also appear to be two people holding hands, symbolizing a close relationship.

This rune typically represents a partnership of sorts—one that is closer than casual friends. Imagine a horse and its rider; each doesn't know the language of the other, yet when riding, it takes only subtle noises and movements for the horse and rider to maneuver quickly and with precision. Together, they can stop on a dime and make quick turns. They take care of each other. That said, this rune can also mean any sort of close relationship—it doesn't have to be of a romantic nature. Regardless, it is less a group of people than a couple working for a common goal.

Ehwaz is also a rune of balance. Each part provides an equal exchange of energy. Balance allows for easier navigation of bumpy roads, tight turns, and pitfalls along the way. Ehwaz also represents motion, so when this rune appears, it could indicate that a journey is at hand, and that you should be prepared to handle sudden changes in the road ahead.

Reversed, Ehwaz can indicate a rift in a partnership, a loss of a loved one, or a time when companionship is desired. It may seem as if there is no forward movement alone, and help is needed to stay on the path. It could mean that there is an issue with a partner, and that to move ahead, these issues need to be addressed.

Look to Ehwaz for balance in a relationship, smooth riding in partnerships, and easy communication with loved ones.

CORRESPONDENCES

GODS: Freya, Freyr, and Frigg

STONES/CRYSTALS: aventurine, halite, and labradorite

HERB: ragwort

COLOR: white

TAROT: The Lovers

PRACTICAL USES

- Invoke Ehwaz during wedding ceremonies and anniversaries for smooth sailing.

- Make a bindrune with Ehwaz and Ansuz as the foundation to communicate with animals or a beloved pet.

- Take the rune Ehwaz with you when traveling as part of a couple, making a bindrune with Raidho for a pleasant journey with your partner.

- Build a bindrune of Berkana, Ehwaz, and Gifu to find a new potential lover or mate.

- Call upon the energies of Ehwaz when working with a partner on a project or event.

Mannaz

PRONUNCIATION: MAN-naz

ALSO KNOWN AS: Man, Manna, and Mathr

SOUND: *m* as in "man"

TRANSLATION: humankind or man

KEYWORDS: connection, group, humanity, humankind, and support

Mannaz is the rune of humankind. It represents the support of a group of people. The symbol looks like two people facing each other, holding each other's hips, or with crossed arms holding hands in a sign of mutual support. This rune can symbolize the support of a group of people, such as coworkers, family, or a circle of friends. It asks us to treat others in your life with respect and maintain a relationship that offers mutual support. A balanced rune, Mannaz represents the contributions of multiple people working in tandem to move forward.

When Mannaz appears in a reading, it could point to a situation involving a group of people. This situation may involve coworkers, friends, or family members. It shows that there is support available or that you have been there for others in ways that are important. Mannaz may be asking you to look to your support group for advice on a situation or help with a personal issue. It may also indicate that the answers you seek are available through others who are involved in your life.

Trying to handle everything yourself when you have a valuable resource in your circle of friends and partners doesn't serve you well. Mannaz offers a collaborative energy and encourages you to work with others toward common goals. Use this rune to guide you and inspire you to offer mutual aid to those in your life who support you.

When Mannaz appears reversed, it could indicate that there are problems with a group of people. Maybe there are issues at work, in the home, or within a circle of friends. There can be feelings of solitude and not being appreciated for your contributions. Mannaz in a reversed position lets you know that you may not get help from others at this time and that you are to maneuver through the situation alone for a reason. Alternatively, Mannaz reversed could be asking you to actively look outside yourself for advice and support. You may be too close to a situation to truly see the answers, so input of others is needed. This could point to a mentor, a class, or a program that you engage in to seek wisdom.

CORRESPONDENCES

GODS: Heimdall, Loki, Mannaz, Odin, and Thor

STONES/CRYSTALS: bumblebee jasper, blue apatite, garnet, halite, and obsidian

HERB: madder

COLORS: dark blue and dark red

TAROT: The Magician

PRACTICAL USES

- Carry the rune Mannaz with you when attending work meetings or conference calls for smooth communication and contribution.

- Create a bindrune of Mannaz, Raidho, and Ansuz for a sigil that will assist when looking for a new career, interviews, or attending classes for higher learning.

- Invoke Mannaz in the home to facilitate a harmonious family environment. Place it over the front door or make a sigil to adorn the wall of your living space.

- Draw Mannaz on your person when wanting to inspire creativity or personal power or when working in a busy public environment.

Laguz

PRONUNCIATION: LAH-gooz

ALSO KNOWN AS: Laaz, Lago, Lagus, and Logr

SOUND: *l* as in "lake"

TRANSLATION: lake, ocean, and water

KEYWORDS: feminine energy, intuition, lake, and water

Laguz represents water in all its forms. As one of the four elements, water is the lifeblood of all living things. Water can be chaotic or serene and shallow or deep. It can be crystal clear or it can be dark with murk. Water is at its best when moving, and stagnant when still. It can support life as well as take it. This rune also represents feminine energy and is associated with the Norse goddess Nerthus.

Laguz reminds us to be like water, flowing freely around obstacles like a bubbling brook. Sometimes, life can look like a pristine lake on a sunny day, but if you look below the surface, you might see a murky depth. Laguz is a rune of intuition. It is a reminder to trust your intuition and to explore what's below the surface.

In a reading, Laguz can represent a woman in a relationship. Depending on the surrounding runes, it can offer insights to a situation involving a partner or yourself. When Laguz appears, consider if any situations in your life are a source of tension and look deeper into your own depth to find the answers and swim with, rather than against, the flow of life.

If reversed, Laguz may indicate that there is an issue with a woman in a relationship or that you are experiencing struggles. It may be telling you that you have been doubting your intuition, and the result has been less than satisfying. It could also confirm feelings of discontent or indicate that stress is coming from constantly trying to swim against the current.

As a rune of intuition and insight, Laguz is ideal for developing your psychic abilities. Invoke the Nerthus and use Laguz to strengthen your instincts to see what is not readily apparent. As a rune of nature and Mother Earth, Laguz can be used to help in healing illness, fostering a smooth pregnancy, and navigating situations without undue tension or injury.

CORRESPONDENCES

GODS: Nerthus and Njord

STONES/CRYSTALS: aquamarine, hagstones, pearl, and rutilated quartz

HERBS: leek, lotus, seaweed, and water lily

COLORS: blue, green, and white

TAROT: The Star

PRACTICAL USES

◆ Meditate with Laguz to develop your intuition. Picture the rune in your mind and imagine it connecting with your inner self to enhance your instincts.

◆ Use Laguz in a candle ritual honoring Njord or Nerthus to promote psychic abilities.

◆ Carry the rune Laguz with you or draw it on you to help you flow in any situation during your day.

◆ Use Laguz when in recovery from illness or during pregnancy to reach optimum health faster.

◆ Take Laguz with you when traveling on water, fishing, or diving to better connect with the element.

Ingwaz

PRONUNCIATION: ING-waz

ALSO KNOWN AS: Enguz, Ing, and Inguz

SOUND: *i* or *ng* as in "ring" or "ringing"

TRANSLATION: seed

KEYWORDS: fertility, Freyr, journey, male, masculinity, new growth, relationships, seed, and sexuality

Ingwaz represents new beginnings, fertility, and the Norse god Freyr. The shape of this rune is actually the diamond in the middle of the symbol, but the rune shape is often shown as dual Xs atop each other. This rune is complex yet has no reverse meaning. It is a symbol of new growth and can be viewed as such. Picture the top X being the tiny leaves of a new sproutling. Then picture the bottom X as the new roots taking hold in the soil. The center is the seed.

Along with fertility and new growth, Ingwaz contains aspects of the runes Gifu and Othala—ancestral roots that offer new growth to current family ties and an equal exchange between two partners. Love, sex, and fertility are all represented in Ingwaz. As Gifu represents sex, self-love, giving, and receiving, Ingwaz can represent all these things, but with a partner, much like the difference between fun, casual sex and the development of a lasting relationship.

Freyr is a god of male sexuality, love, fertility, and the growth of a harvest. In fact, the rune Ingwaz looks very similar to a DNA helix. This showcases its connection to life-giving energies and generational, as well as spiritual, growth.

In a reading, Ingwaz can indicate a time of new growth. Something has been planted and is now starting to sprout. This could be a project, relationship, or career. This rune offers a distinctive male or sun energy, and could appear when love is blossoming or sexuality is the focus.

Ingwaz is also a very balanced rune. Relationships and new beginnings usually take the cooperation and equal exchange of a partner or partners. Look for the balance in any situation to ensure that things are ideal for new growth.

CORRESPONDENCES

GODS: Freyr and Ing

STONES/CRYSTALS: amber, moss agate, quartz, rhodonite, rose quartz, and tree agate

HERBS: banana, dragon's blood, pine, and self-heal

COLOR: yellow

TAROT: Judgment

PRACTICAL USES

◆ Meditate with Ingwaz when developing new projects or entering into new potential relationships.

◆ Use Ingwaz in rituals to promote fertility.

◆ Create a couple's candle ritual to Freyr using Ingwaz for maintaining love, lust, happiness, and trust with your partner.

◆ Employ Ingwaz for help with issues of sexuality and potency.

◆ Use Ingwaz when making bread or brewing beer for the family to promote growth and prosperity.

Dagaz

PRONUNCIATION: DAH-gaz

ALSO KNOWN AS: Daaz, Daeg, and Dag

SOUND: *d* as in "dawn"

TRANSLATION: daybreak

KEYWORDS: balance, dawn, day, new start, and sun cycle

Dagaz is the dawn rune—the rune of daybreak and the cycle of the sun. It is a very balanced rune with a shape similar to the infinity symbol. It is always moving forward, never in reverse. It can also appear as a set of butterfly wings, signifying a new beginning or transformation.

Dagaz is tied to the winter solstice and the cycle of night to day. In the North, when winters are cold and nights are long, the sun is a welcome sight and a way to track the season. A rune of energy and sunlight, Dagaz is the power that keeps us moving; it's the motivation that drives us and keeps us waking up each day.

When Dagaz appears in a reading, it can indicate that a brighter day is ahead. Much like Kenaz and Sowilo, this is a rune of fire and light. Dagaz is about hope and determination. Better times are coming or are at hand, as Dagaz offers us a cycle of light to enjoy.

Regarding new beginnings, the butterfly-like shape of Dagaz reminds us that each new day offers another chance to become a better person. Enjoy the cycle of daily life and realize it as a true gift.

In magic, Dagaz can represent a doorway or portal. One can use it at the beginning and end of rituals or magical workings to open and close the ceremony. It is also a transformative rune that can be called upon to manifest change in the future, both physically or spiritually.

As there is no reverse for Dagaz, when it appears alongside negative runes or at a time when days are arduous, it's calling you to look deeper. It indicates that a better time is coming if you have the courage to navigate the darkness. It could also help inspire a new beginning of sorts. Maybe there is a new cycle on the horizon, but you just can't see it yet.

CORRESPONDENCES

GODS: Astara, Heimdall, and Odin

STONES/CRYSTALS: bumblebee jasper, carnelian, fire agate, and ouro verde quartz

HERB: clary sage

COLOR: light blue

TAROT: Temperance

PRACTICAL USES

◆ Use Dagaz for opening and closing magical workings, rituals, and ceremonies.

◆ Employ Dagaz when going through a transition of any kind by carving or writing it on a candle or meditating with the rune.

◆ Trace the rune over your heart when feeling a lack of energy or during illness. Focus on the healing energy of Dagaz and let it offer warmth and inspiration to your day.

◆ Use Dagaz in a bindrune with Ingwaz or Fehu to inspire a cycle of growth and abundance.

Othala

PRONUNCIATION: OH-tha-la

ALSO KNOWN AS: Odil, Othel, and Othila

SOUND: *o* as in "oval"

TRANSLATION: ancestry

KEYWORDS: ancestral roots, family, heritage, home, and legacy

Othala is the rune of ancestral roots, of family and heritage. It can represent an inheritance of wealth, land, or legacy. It can also represent the passing down of family traits, knowledge, and ancestral history. The symbol of the rune looks a lot like the roof of a home, with the lower legs as the ancestral roots. Othala incorporates the symbols of Gifu as well as Ingwaz, runes that represent equal exchange and growth. Both of these aspects are part of a happy household and prosperous lineage.

Othala can also represent the knowledge of tribal or family elders. Stories passed down from generation to generation can keep the values and histories of a family alive. Othala is also representative of a mentor or mentorship, and the attainment of knowledge through another who has more wisdom and experience. In today's world, there are many ways of passing along information electronically. But Othala reminds us that human connection is the key to a lasting legacy. It calls on you to connect with others to orally pass along stories, lessons, and insights.

In a reading, Othala could point to matters of the home. In a forward position, it might indicate a need to lean on family members for insights and wisdom. Depending on the surrounding runes and the situation, Othala can be a reminder to also look to your extended family and circle of friends for assistance or support. There may be someone close to you with valuable advice to pass down. Othala puts the focus on the home and family.

Reversed, Othala could indicate problems on the home front. The family setting may be disrupted, or there could be issues with an extended family member. As Othala is also a rune of protection, it can appear if you are not feeling safe in your own home or if you feel vulnerable there. This could relate to a situation between parents and children or siblings and partners. Regardless, Othala in reverse is a confirmation that the family tree is getting a shakedown.

As the last rune in the Elder Futhark, Othala concludes our runic journey. It is the hearth that warms us and welcomes us home. It inspires us to create a happy and thriving home.

CORRESPONDENCES

GOD: Odin

STONES/CRYSTALS: tree agate and amethyst

HERBS: basil, alfalfa, hawthorn, and clover

COLOR: deep yellow

TAROT: The Moon

PRACTICAL USES

◆ Create a talisman using Othala to hang over the entryway to your home for protection and happiness within the family.

◆ Trace Othala on the dashboard of your car to protect you from getting pulled over.

◆ Use Othala in a candle ritual to help overcome issues within the family or household, for protection of family members, or to honor those who have passed.

◆ Carry Othala with you when going to classes or learning from a mentor.

Tyr's Ætt shows us the benefits of human connection. It is a set of runes that focuses on relationships, not only with others, but with ourselves as well. This ætt highlights friends, family, lovers, and mentors. We learn through the teachings of others as well as our own experiences. Most of the runes in Tyr's Ætt are balanced runes. Find the commonalities between these runes and take the lessons of balance to help overcome obstacles. This includes the balance of your spirit as well as balance among friends, family members, and partners. Also, remember that:

- New beginnings can be found in Berkana, Ingwaz, and Dagaz.

- Legal issues can be helped through the use of Tiwaz, as it is the rune of legalities and fairness.

- The support of friends, family members, and partners is represented in the runes of Ingwaz, Mannaz, and Ehwaz.

- All of these runes can be used in rituals that promote fertility, prosperity, love, and harmony.

- This is the last set of runes in the Elder Futhark. The last in this set is Othala, which leads the runic road back home to our family and ancestry.

PART III

Using Runes for Divination and Magic

Runes are the most versatile tools for divination and magic. There are many ways to use these simple symbols in daily practice, from gaining insight to creating powerful talismans. In this section of the book, you will discover all the ways to begin and continue your journey in runework.

As you read through this part, remember that you can add your own perspectives and work with what resonates with you. Once your journey takes you into magical practice, the runes will guide you to what works best, what you have around you, and what energies inspire you most. Find the tools that work with your space and lifestyle. Don't feel nervous that you may do something wrong. Rather, focus on your intuition and bring runework into your life in a way that suits your needs.

This is called a practice for a reason. It takes time and patience to develop a strong sense of what messages the runes are offering. As you develop your divination skills, the runes may take on different meanings. You may have epiphanies that bring new light to certain runes, or you may develop your own way of casting or presenting layouts. Embrace your unique path.

CHAPTER SEVEN

Choosing a Rune Set

This is a practical chapter that explores how to choose, make, and care for your runes. The following sections will answer some of the most common questions new rune-workers ask.

Runes are the tools and you are the magic. Your rune sets should be considered sacred artifacts that you treat with respect and reverence. By treating these tools in this way, you will develop a ritualistic sense that helps bring intention and power to spells and rituals. The fact is that your runes are simple pieces of wood, stone, or other material. They are not magical in themselves, but are the conduits for magical work. You make them magical by treating them as such.

Here, you will learn how to treat runes as magical artifacts and how to use them in various ways to expand your spiritual practice. A rune-worker may have many different sets of runes, each with its own personality and specific purpose. One set may be for personal use only, and another for divination for others. Some runes are ideal for casting, and others more suited for layouts or carrying. The options are limited only by your own creativity and intuition.

Finding a Rune Set

Choosing a first rune set can be daunting for some. There are many styles of rune sets commercially available, both in metaphysical stores as well as online. These sets are commonly made from wood, stones, resin, and bone.

There are many opinions on how to choose runes, and for anyone looking for a new set, take all the advice given with an open mind. Runes for divination are a modern construct, so there are no hard-and-fast rules. Runes can be made of any material, and it's perfectly acceptable to purchase any rune set that you are called to. We'll cover making your own set later in this chapter.

You may own several rune sets, as each may have a different purpose. When choosing a set, take into consideration how it will be used, what material it is made from, and the size and shape of the staves.

Most types of runes may be used for casting. For layouts, more uniform, flat shapes work best. Stone runes are ideal for carrying individually, as you can focus on the power of the rune as well as the energy of the stone. Round runes when cast on a table may roll off, and thicker runes may have a more satisfying feel when tossed on a rune cloth. Large runes may be easier for some to see, but mini runes are ideal for travel.

Let your intuition guide you. Hold sets when you can and experience how they feel in your hand. See if you get tingles or if you can't stop holding them. You'll make the right choice no matter what set you pick.

Making Your Own Runes

Runestaves can be made from almost any material. You will find them made out of bone, horn, leather, metal, paper, plastic, polymer clay, shell, stone, and wood. Accepting that runes can be made from anything allows the option to choose material that speaks to you.

No matter how many sets of runes you purchase, making your own set is pretty special. The act of choosing your material, carefully drawing out, and then carving, painting, or burning each rune onto the staves is a rewarding experience. Even if you don't consider yourself a crafter or maker, you should find materials that suit your skill level. You do not have to make these runes your main set, as making runes is part of learning their secrets. Crafting a set of runes is an opportunity to ritualize your studies, activate your internal power, and spend time learning what each rune means to you.

Ritualize the crafting of the runes by finding a creative space to make them. Lay out your materials and create a sacred crafting space. Paint the rune symbols with a power color. Red traditionally represents blood, but feel free to use whatever color you feel works with your set. Find a bag or vessel to make a sacred home for these runes. When you complete the crafting and consecration of your own runes, you will feel a difference. You will have completed a very important part of your rune studies and will be prepared to dive even deeper into the mysteries of these symbols.

Runescripts and Bindrunes

As mentioned previously, runes are one of the most versatile tools of magic. Another way to enjoy this versatility is in creating runescripts and bindrunes for yourself or others.

A runescript is a line of runes set in a certain order that creates an intentional message. These can be created in a number of ways, such as written out on paper or carved into wood or stone. Runescripts typically feature a balanced number of runes—traditionally, three, six, or nine runes—but feel free to experiment. These runes tell the story of what the intention is. Runescripts should be created in a ritual setting using ceremony to bring them to life.

Once the runescript is created, it can be used in a ritual, carried for its intended purpose, or set in a place where the intentions are to be fulfilled. For example, a runescript of Fehu, Gifu, Jera, Othala, and Wunjo tells a story and sets intention. Fehu brings in wealth and abundance, and Gifu is used for mutual exchange and to tie the runescript together. Meanwhile, Jera represents a harvest of the home, and Othala provides a focus on the home. Wunjo at the end signifies the joy and satisfaction gained through this process.

A bindrune is a series of runes that are combined into a single symbol known as a sigil. Bindrunes can be drawn on the skin, made as talismans for protection, or used in runic spellwork. Creating a bindrune is as simple as picking out three runes and drawing them together into one symbol. You can use as many runes as you like, but too many make a cluttered bindrune. You may notice other runes appear as well. Get creative and have fun with this process.

You can create your own personal bindrune by using your name. Pick out the runes that correspond with your name or initials, and see how they fit together into a single symbol. Use this as your own signature bindrune in your journals or as a personal power sigil.

Rune Care

Each set of runes should be considered a sacred artifact and treated with respect and honor. This allows you to bring reverence to a reading or ritual using the runes.

As runes are tools of the rune-worker, allowing them to channel energies through the staves to access insight, some enjoy ritually cleansing and charging their runes. Many like to consecrate new rune sets to attune to them and develop a bond with each set. You can develop your own special ways of attuning to them, using this book as your guide. Feel free to make any additions that resonate with your personal practice and enjoy the process. Occasionally, you may feel the need to cleanse or "clean" your runes, such as after performing multiple readings for others. Many rune-workers also cleanse new rune sets.

Cleansing can be performed in many ways. A simple way to cleanse a rune set is to pass them through sage, then through incense smoke, asking Freya to bless them while doing so. Another way to cleanse runes is to put them in a bag and place the bag in a bowl that is filled with salt. Kosher, sea, black, or Himalayan pink salt will work for this purpose.

Selenite is a soft, white stone that is readily available at most crystal shops. Selenite is a cleansing stone that doesn't hold on to anyone's energy and doesn't need to be cleaned or charged. It can be used to clean your own aura from energies that are not yours, and it can do the same for your rune set. Simply place the rune set in a selenite bowl or plate, or pass a selenite wand over it to clear off any negative energy.

Consecrating Runes

Welcome any new rune set into your universe with a rune consecration ritual or ceremony. The process of consecrating a rune set helps you connect your spirit to the energies of the runes. Consecrating your runes turns them from simple staves or stones into powerful artifacts that will help you on your journey. This also starts your relationship to these runes and will help you connect when using them. After consecration, be sure to treat them as respected artifacts, time-honored tools, and trusted friends.

To consecrate a rune set, first set a sacred space. You may set out effigies of the gods, crystals, and any other artifacts or offerings you use for ritual. Light a candle for protection. Pour out all the runes into a bowl. Take each rune in your hand and say its name aloud, placing it back into the bag after doing so. When each stave has been recognized, pass the set through sage smoke, asking Freya, Odin, and any other deities that appeal to you to bless your runes. Then pass them through incense to bring them joyful energy. An extended version includes tying a colored string around the set nine times and letting it sit on the altar overnight. In the morning, untie the rune bag and breathe onto it, giving it life, intention, and a welcome place in your practice.

Feel free to add any ritualistic prayers, intentions, poems, and offerings to this ceremony. This is about how you intend to treat your artifacts and how you can honor the runes and their mysteries.

Charging Runes

Some rune-workers like to charge their runes, giving them a boost of energy. You can do this if the runes haven't been used often, or if they feel like they need a little pick-me-up. In the same manner as charging crystals, runes can be charged to imbue them with your own energy. You can also charge them after each reading, using an intentional prayer or blessing. Another way to charge runes is to set them out under a full moon, much like you would do with crystals and stones. This is especially helpful if the runes are made of actual stones or crystals.

To charge runes with crystals, simply surround your rune set with stones that offer the energies you wish to bring to the setting. Clear quartz, amethyst, and other high-vibrational crystals work well for this. Use a wand, crystal, or finger to direct the energies from the crystals to the runes while offering your own intentions and energy to refresh your runes, enhancing your own attunement, or personal connection, to them.

During your charging ceremony, call to the higher powers that direct the mysteries of the runes. Feel free to call upon Odin and Freya to bless them with their energies. Use your own intentions to send good, positive, and healing energies into them. State any intentions aloud or chant the names of the runes as you charge them.

Charge runes as much as you see fit. Create your own ritual for charging runes and have fun with it. Make it a part of your practice, and enjoy the benefits of bonding to each set of runes you own.

Discovering a Set's Personality

When you have consecrated your runes and are ready to begin incorporating them into your practice, you can start to attune to them. Attunement is the process of creating a deeper connection to these tools. Using your intention and connective energies, you can enjoy accurate readings and enhanced understanding of the messages received through your runes.

There are many ways to attune to runes. A simple method is to carry them with you as much as possible. Have them next to you when you sleep, and spend a couple weeks laying them out and tracing the runes with your finger. Studying their meanings while holding them or laying them out in front of you is also a way to attune to them.

Meditating with each rune builds a connection with your runes as well as spirit guides and those who will offer you messages through them. By holding each rune and meditating on its meaning, you can ask it to help you understand it. Pay attention to any visions that come to mind and thank each rune when finished.

Practice with them by simply laying them out or casting them. Notice how they feel in your hand and how their shape lends to any certain way of casting. When holding them, make the intention to put your energy into them and connect with their energy. Put your love and compassion into the set as a whole and appreciate the beauty and uniqueness of your rune set.

You might get the feeling that a rune set wants to be used in a certain way. You might feel one set is good for use on others, but another set should be used only for yourself. You might use another rune set strictly for grids or intention layouts. You might even have a family set you crafted for use when consulting for your family members.

Give yourself time to attune. This can take anywhere from three days to a couple weeks, depending on how much time and energy you spend on the process.

KEY TAKEAWAYS

Bonding with a new rune set is a powerful experience. In this chapter, you discovered ways to make a rune set a truly magical artifact. Each set has a personality and purpose, making runes a versatile tool of magic. Each rune-worker is unique as well, so know that however you choose to perform rituals of cleansing, consecration, or charging the runes, it's okay to bring in your own spin on the practice. Whether you make a set, purchase one, or are gifted runes, you can make them your own through consecration and attunement. Also, remember:

- Rune sets can be purchased, gifted, or made. Each set has a purpose and should be cared for like they are powerful artifacts.

- Charging and consecration allow runes to be attuned to your energies.

- Making a rune set is an important part of the learning process and helps you focus on the meanings while adding intention to the set.

- Attuning to the runes offers a deeper insight and allows you to intuitively see the messages being sent through them.

CHAPTER EIGHT

How to Cast Runes

Casting runes is a rewarding experience, though it can be intimidating at first, as this journey has many twists and turns. Like any practice, divination takes time and patience. In this chapter, you'll find information for beginning your rune rituals, what tools and items you'll need for a cast or layout, and how to prepare yourself and your space for ritual and ceremony.

Reading runes for others is a completely different experience from doing it for yourself and should be done only after you have studied the runes and reading techniques thoroughly. When casting for yourself, answers tend to come more intuitively, as you know aspects of yourself that you will recognize in a cast. When divining for others, a conversation is needed to discover why some runes appear the way they do.

A rune-worker can choose from various casting techniques, layout options, and divination methods. Experiment to find what resonates with you. Don't worry about doing it wrong at first. Just keep casting and doing your best to interpret the meanings. As you progress in your practice, the runes will start to appear more like messages. Use your intuition and trust that your cosmic connection is strong.

Gather the Essentials

If you are just getting started with the runes, there are a few basic items you can use in your practice. If you are weaving runework into an existing divination practice, you may already have many tools at your disposal. The following are some commonly recommended items for your altar or ritual space.

ARTIFACTS AND STATUARY: Add artifacts to a ceremonial altar or other sacred statuary to call in certain gods. This adds visual appeal and creates a focal point. Artifacts that are sacred or represent other spiritual aspects can be placed to bring their intentions and honor to the space.

CANDLES: Three candles can be used to represent Urd, Verdandi, and Skuld, the three Norns that represent the past, present, and future. Other candles can be added to represent colors of the gods, intentions, and protection.

FOCUS TOOLS: When consecrating a space, altar, or artifact, use focus tools like wands, swords, and knives. These are ceremonial in nature and are activated during rituals. For instance, you can use a wand to activate a bindrune, a knife to create a sacred circle, and a sword to create a ward of protection on a wall or in a doorway.

INCENSE AND BURNERS: You will need a way to burn incense. When burning incense, it doesn't matter whether it is in stick or powder form. If using a burner and charcoal, you can grind incense and sage to easily sprinkle atop the coal.

JOURNAL: It is important to chronicle your journey. Find a journal that you want to use as a partner in your journey, something you don't have to share with anyone else if you don't want to.

RUNE CLOTH: This can be a simple blank cloth (made or purchased) of any color or material that calls to you. It is mainly used to create a focal point for practice and to keep your runes protected from hard surfaces. Adorning or choosing the pattern for your rune cloth is up to you, as this is part of your intention and personal ritual work.

STONES AND CRYSTALS: When setting up an altar or sacred space, you can add a variety of stones to enhance rituals or energies and to help attract power and provide protection.

Creating a Sacred Space

Before you begin, create a sacred space in which to work. This can be any space in which you happen to be, whether in your own home, a friend's space, or even the retail store at which you do readings. Creating a sacred space can be done anywhere and is an important part of the process.

To create this space, first set the stage. You can do this a number of ways, such as by shaking a rattle to disperse negativity from the space, burning sage and incense to cleanse it, or playing meditative music to put you in the mood.

Adorn your altar or table setting with things that make it feel special. Place your rune cloth down and set your candles. Feel free to add any other items you might want to use for aesthetics or as representations of your intentions. Statuaries, antlers, bones, feathers, herbs, and crystals can all help make your personal space even more special.

Once your space is set, thank the universe and ask for spirit to protect it and use it as a realm of communication for your greater good. You can use a wand or knife to cast a circle of protection around your space. Whether simple or elaborately adorned, your space is sacred and protected. It is *your* space and should feel comfortable and inspiring.

Set Your Intentions

Whether or not your conscious mind believes in the power of intention, your subconscious mind and higher self does. Intention is the real magic. Of all the advice given in this book and all the freedom offered in how to practice your runework, it is the power of intention that is most important. Intention is the energy of the subconscious mind following directions from the conscious mind, without the conscious mind being aware of it.

To properly work with divination, you must accept that conscious intention activates energies in yourself. Those energies transfer to the runes and create the connection to the higher self and spirit. When combined, your thoughts and actions activate your magic, producing results based on your thoughts and intention. This is an example of the conscious and subconscious working in tandem.

When you pick up the runes and speak to them, asking for them to connect with spirit and offer an accurate reading, you are using your intention to open that connection to the divine. When you lay out a ritual site and recite prayers, light candles, burn incense, and hail the gods, you are enhancing your intentions with actions.

You will use intention when making runes, when crafting bindrunes and runestaves, and when performing divination. Intentions will drive your spellwork and rituals. Intention is used for cleansing, grounding, and protection. Get used to trusting in your intentions and knowing what it feels like to use them. You will start to see yourself change the way you speak, think, and act.

Prepare for a Casting

Part of your runework preparations should always include cleansing and grounding. This offers you a way to relieve yourself of any energies that are not yours before moving forward with your rune-work. One way to do this is by sitting with both feet on the ground and repeating this phrase out loud or in your mind: "I release any energy that is not mine." Say this three times and imagine all the energies you may have accumulated from others draining down your body and into the floor. See how you feel after as you visualize this cleansing micro meditation.

Use a selenite wand to wipe away negative energies. Start at the top of your head, waving the wand in a sweeping motion a few inches from your body. This will cleanse your aura. Wipe in a downward motion as if you were whisking away water from your skin. Selenite does not hold other energies and does not need cleansing or cleaning.

You can use a wand or other selenite item to do this as well. However you cleanse and ground, do this before and after your activity to balance out energies and give you a clearer vision of your intentions.

Casting Runes

Before you begin casting runes, you will need to choose a casting technique. Casting is only one of various ways of using runes for divination. This method is ideal for quick answers. As you study and practice, you will find what rune-casting technique you feel most comfortable with. Feel free to create your own versions of casting or tossing runes.

Some runes are well suited for casting, and others are less so. For example, round runes may have a tendency to roll out of bounds or off the table when you drop or toss them lightly onto your surface. Meanwhile, runes made from a thin, super-lightweight material may not travel far enough to land where they should on your surface. Use what feels right for each technique, but be mindful of the construction of your runes and how that may impact a reading.

Remember to cleanse, ground, and protect when casting runes. Call in your spirit guides to help bring you the needed insights. You can practice rune casting just by tossing or dropping the runes without any intention. This will allow you to practice your techniques without disrupting your universe.

◇◇◇◇ Circle/Spiral

There are a few ways to read runes for divination. The ones featured here are easy, useful, and accurate ways to get a reading, making them excellent for beginners. Layouts are another, yet very different, way of performing rune divination. These techniques are most often used when not performing other layouts. Many times, layouts and their explanations are inhibiting to those learning to use the runes. You may choose to experiment with complex layouts as you gain more experience, but simplicity will always serve you well in this case.

◆ Lay out a rune cloth that has a circle drawn in the center of it (about twelve to fifteen inches across).

◆ Choose nine runes, or, alternatively, just grab a handful of runes—it doesn't matter how many.

◆ Offer an intentional prayer or ask your question while holding the runes in your hands.

◆ Let the runes drop from about twelve inches above the cloth.

◆ Discard the runes that fell facing down or any that are outside of the circle.

◆ Start from the center of the circle for the rune order and work your way out in an imaginary spiral.

◆ Read any runes facing inward as reversed; runes facing outward can be considered to be in the forward position.

◆ Tip: Create a rune cloth that has a spiral and use it for a guide to reading the runes in the proper time line, as well as whether forward or reversed.

◇◇◇◇ Rune Toss

◆ Place the rune cloth on a wide table or on the floor.

◆ Pick nine runes at random or just grab a handful.

◆ Speak your intentions and ask the question to which you are seeking answers.

◆ Toss the runes away from you, letting them fall in a linear pattern.

◆ Discard any runes that are facing down.

◆ Read runes facing away from you as being in the forward position, and runes facing your direction as reversed.

◆ Interpret the runes closest to you as relating to the past, the ones in the middle as the present, and those farthest away as the future.

Reversed Runes

The use and concept of reversed runes was influenced by the tarot system of divination. Reading reversed runes is still a modern practice from what we know historically, and some opt not to read runes as reversed at all. Inexperienced rune-workers can be intimidated by reversed runes, as they don't want to see them in their own readings. But reversed runes don't automatically spell out doom and gloom. They are another way to receive messages and insight. They can bring light to issues that need attention, offer a warning to what may come if not prepared, and provide confirmation that aspects of your life are offering challenges.

If you are looking to get a quick answer to a question, you might cast or lay out a rune. If it is forward, the answer is yes, and in reverse, the answer is no. This works with any rune that can be reversed, and the actual rune meaning should be taken into consideration.

If you have a reading layout of several runes and you have many reversed ones, look at their position and inquire why they are reversed if it is not apparent. These reversed runes may indicate an issue in various areas that need attention, while the surrounding runes will explore the insight, guidance, or confirmation of the overall reading.

Reversed runes in a future time line may offer a warning as to what may come, calling on you to be prepared for the challenge to avoid negative outcomes. For example, Fehu reversed in the future doesn't mean you will come into poverty and despair. It may simply be a heads-up that a time is coming soon when finances will be tight and saving now can help keep your abundance in the future.

When reading for others, inquire about reversed runes if the answer is not apparent. When reading for yourself, you'll usually know why a rune is reversed. If that information isn't initially apparent, trust that the meaning will make itself known with some truthful introspection.

Don't be afraid of or confused by reversed runes in a reading. Study the reversed meanings as much as the forward meanings to learn why they appear. Use them as another means of cosmic communication when the forward meaning of the rune doesn't apply.

KEY TAKEAWAYS

Rune casting is fulfilling in many ways. It can help you make decisions, find inspiration, gain insight, and offer helpful guidance. In this chapter, we started the practical journey with runes, covering the tools of the trade and options for casting and layout techniques. The key to good divination is trusting your intuition, which can be the most challenging aspect. As you get ready for what comes next, remember:

◆ Getting prepped for your journey with the proper tools is important. Candles, runes, a rune cloth, and other inspirational items set the stage for rune readings.

◆ Intentions unlock your magic. It is important to set intentions first for rune readings and other rune rituals.

◆ Creating a sacred space offers spiritual protection, cosmic connection, and an inspired practice.

◆ There are several things to consider when casting runes. These include time line, layout patterns, and casting techniques. Each has its benefits and place in rune readings. Reversed runes can offer valuable guidance for addressing difficult questions and expand readings with greater vision.

CHAPTER NINE

Understanding Rune Spreads

This chapter introduces the use of rune spreads. Spreads are different from casting as they present a layout of runes in a specific order in a specific time line.

The foundational spread is a simple three-rune layout of past, present, and future. Along with the standard nine-rune layout, this is the most common, but there are many to choose from. Some are simple, and others are more complex, delving into the various aspects of our humanity and heavily influenced by the practice of tarot.

Layouts are a great place to start for those who are already familiar with tarot. These spreads can be customized. For example, a quick reading for one person may require only a three-rune spread for checking in, and a couple might need an extended layout with specific areas of interest to gain answers from a reading.

Read through the layouts and practice reading each. See what resonates with you and discover any elements you may wish to add or remove. The simplicity of the runes, paired with the complexity of a well-thought-out spread, make for impactful readings that offer in-depth insight for yourself and others.

Gaining Insight from Rune Spreads

Rune spreads and runic layouts offer a definitive way to examine life in a past, present, and future context. Extended spreads offer ways to define specific aspects and issues you are working on. In a rune spread, the runes are presented facedown and turned over.

It is during the shuffling process that the cosmic forces intervene and guide your hands when choosing the runes for a layout. Once placed, turn them over to reveal a forward or reversed orientation and relate them with their position.

Runic layouts also offer an opportunity for conversation. It's not about telling someone's future, but rather about defining issues and challenges through discussion. Spreads offer a way to pinpoint a certain issue and discover what insight other runes have to help overcome obstacles. When arranged in a layout, the runes take on another life. They start to form a story that is easy to understand.

During readings, make sure to journal your layouts and readings for others. Take photos of the runes in the spread and refer back to them after time to see how accurate they were and how they helped.

Single-Rune Spread

A single-rune spread is a quick way to consult the runes and get a simple answer. This can be an answer to a question or an insight to your day. If asking a question, be as specific as possible to gain the simplest answer a single rune can offer. A single-rune pull can also be implemented to extend the reading of another, longer rune spread or to answer yes-or-no questions.

One of the best ways to learn the meanings of the runes is to experience them daily. Pulling a single rune and taking it on your day can be a wonderful experience. To do this, simply ask aloud "What rune should I study today?" and pull a single rune from your bag. As you move through the day, you will start to notice aspects of the rune you pulled. You may see the rune in the trees and in buildings or experience a situation defined by that rune. Document your rune pulls in a journal and put yourself on a program of learning by simply pulling a single rune every day for thirty days.

◇◇◇◇ *Odin's Eye*

Gain insight to an issue by asking, "Odin, master of the runes, which rune should I study to gain insight on my situation?"

Pull a single rune from the rune bag and read descriptions of its meaning from a few sources. Find the nuggets of insight within the meanings to discern what message it might be offering.

◇◇◇◇ *Yes or No*

If you would like a quick answer to a question, you can consult a single rune. Much like flipping a coin, this method offers an answer of yes or no, while still bringing insight to the question at hand.

To perform this, simply ask the question and pull a single rune from the bag. If the rune is generally considered positive, the answer is yes. If it is a rune that is generally associated with strife or challenges, the answer is no. Another version of this is to take out any rune and toss it onto the rune cloth after asking the question. If the rune lands faceup, the answer is yes. If facedown, the answer is no.

Two-Rune Spread

This spread requires two runes to answer a specific question. First, picture the question in your mind or say it out loud. Choose two runes and lay them out in their upright position. This is not about reading the runes forward or reverse, but rather as two separate aspects of the reading.

Two runes is not a lot to go on for answers, and digging into the descriptions may be necessary to discern the message offered. This layout is also not recommended for extremely important decisions that could impact others.

◇◇◇◇ *Hugin and Munin*

THE POSITIVE **THE NEGATIVE**

Hugin and Munin were Odin's ravens. They flew around the nine worlds and brought back news of all the goings-on in the realms. Hugin meant "Thought" and Munin was "Memory." It is often thought of as a favorable sign to see a raven or crow flying over. Viking warriors knew that Odin was with them and strived to succeed in battle when ravens appeared.

The first rune represents the positive, or pros, of the question at hand. The second rune represents the negative, or cons, of the situation. If the question is regarding a job offer and you want to gain insight into whether you should accept, this layout may offer some wisdom. For example, if Fehu and Othala are drawn in response to the question, Fehu appearing in the first position could be indicating that one of the benefits is the increase in income. Othala in the second position, or con, could indicate that you may need to make sacrifices on the home front to maintain the new schedule.

Three-Rune Spread

The three-rune spread is one of the most common and simple ways to get a quick assessment of your situation. The first two runes offer a confirmation of the past, as well as where you are now. The last rune offers insight on what to expect in the near future.

Take all three runes into account and consider how they relate to each other to better understand the message. The first rune is the past, and may offer insight to the next rune, which is where you are now. The last rune is the future aspect and can show what may be coming in the near future and/or advice on how to approach the next part of your journey.

◇◇◇◇ *Three Norns (Past, Present, and Future)*

THE RECENT PAST   **THE PRESENT**   **THE NEAR FUTURE**

In Norse mythology, the Three Norns who weave the Web of Wyrd—Urd, Verdandi, and Skuld—at the foot of the world tree, Yggdrasil, represent what has been, what is now, and what will be.

To perform this layout, set the stage, make your intentions, pour out the runes, and turn them all facedown. Choose three runes. Lay them out upside down and side by side. Turn them over like a book to get a forward or reverse orientation.

You can modify this layout to accommodate other intentions as well. Just be specific with your intentions and designations of which layout you use. Following are two examples of ways to designate three-rune spreads for a variety of reading options. Use the same methodology for preparing your reading as above. Let's say you want a spiritual check-in, with a quick reading on where you stand currently in your life.

FEHU (REVERSED): With Fehu reversed in the past position, you may have gone through a period of little abundance. Finances may have been the focus in the recent past, and career options may have been limited.

NAUTHIZ: Nauthiz represents basic human needs. In this position, the focus is to get needs met. This may mean searching for a new career or that there is another need to fill that is keeping you from moving forward.

EIHWAZ: Eihwaz in the future position may indicate that there is a time in the near future when you will have to let go of things that don't serve you. Examine your life to see what is no longer a positive influence and find ways to let it go. This could be a personal attitude, a stagnant relationship, or a bad habit. Make the choices that best encourage your growth.

Four-Rune Spread

This spread uses four runes to gain balanced insight on a current situation. Using this layout brings intention to a specific issue or situation and a light to influences that shape your decisions regarding challenging issues, whether you realize it or not. Influences can guide, misdirect, or offer confirmation in a reading. Look to them to understand what the best way to move forward may be. This spread can be laid out side by side in a linear fashion, starting with Position 1 on the left and moving to the right. On the next page we will look at at a four-rune spread for a The Hand of Tyr reading.

| The true focus of the situation | What is influencing the situation | The counter-balance of the situation | What to keep in mind navigating the situation |

The Hand of Tyr is called that because like the previous spread, it, too, focuses on balance. Tyr is the god of justice, fairness, balance, and legal issues. The myth tells of how he lost his hand when the wolf Fenrir took it. So he is the one-handed god.

LAGUZ (REVERSED): Laguz reversed may point to your current state. Even if you think the issue is with the partner, this position states that the true issue is with you. Laguz reversed indicates self-doubt, feeling overwhelmed, and being at the mercy of ego and emotion.

THURISAZ: Thurisaz in this position may indicate that ego and emotions have taken hold. Opinions are set and kept solid in conversation. Thurisaz is a rune of power, indicating that maybe you are not leaving room for any other opinions, all due to ego keeping you from realizing the imbalance of the situation and finding a higher perspective.

GIFU: Gifu in this position means that an equal exchange is needed. Things are imbalanced and someone is taking too much while the other is too aggressive. Gifu is a rune of give-and-take, of partnership and love. It is a sign that finding the balance in a situation and coming together with a heartfelt energy will yield better results than butting heads. Be aware of when conversations start to fall too far one way or the other. Gifu asks for an equal energetic exchange.

ANSUZ: Ansuz is the rune of communication in all forms. It asks you to take a higher perspective on the situation and see things for what they truly are. If communication starts to break down, redirect. Seek wisdom from past arguments to figure out how to navigate the situation without aggressive emotions. In this position, Ansuz indicates that with proper communication, both sides will more clearly understand the other and be able to come to a mutually beneficial resolution.

Nine-Rune Spread

Nine is a sacred number to the Norse and has deep meanings in the cosmology of our universe. A nine-rune spread offers an extended reading that delves deeper into the issues and insight.

There are several ways to use a nine-rune spread, and each method assigns different meanings to each position. When using this many runes for divination, particularly for another person, it's important to use conversation to discover why the runes are in their given positions. If a rune comes up reversed and there is no apparent reason, talk to the querent to find out why it's reversed. Many times, the runes are there to pull out issues that have gone unnoticed or were not the original focus of the reading.

Explain the positions of the layout with clarity and keep the story flowing without overwhelming the querent with expanded meanings on each rune. The reading might just point out the obvious, and a consultation reveals why the runes are offering the message. If reading solo, be truthful to your higher self. Take the time to truly study the reading and discern its insight.

◇◇◇◇ *Hagal's Snowflake*

Hagal's Snowflake is so called because the name means "hail," and this layout can look like a snowflake, with its eight points and intersecting connections, as you will see on the next page. This is an expanded version of the three-rune spread. It offers a middle row of three focus runes for past, present, and future. The two outside rows of runes are the influencers to the focus runes. The influencing runes can often indicate why the focus rune is what it is. They can shed light on what was causing issues, how you are dealing with situations, and what may influence an outcome. One side is the personal influence, and the other is an outside influence on the issue.

To create this spread, set the intention and pick the runes at random, assigning them to any position intuitively. Read the layout from bottom to top, with the lower middle rune being the past, the middle representing the now, and the top focus rune as the future possibility. Reveal the runes one by one, turning them over like a book. Offer a brief explanation of each as you go, starting with the past and its influencers. Then move to the now and lastly the future focus rune and its influencers.

Let's say that you have a querent who simply wanted a check-in, or rather, a general reading with no specific question. Remember, the descriptions here are only part of the divination process. The other half comes from you tuning in to the querent, as well as open conversations regarding situations. The runes are read from bottom to top, starting with the focus rune on the lower row. After that is turned over, read the rune to its left, then right. Repeat for the middle and top rows of runes.

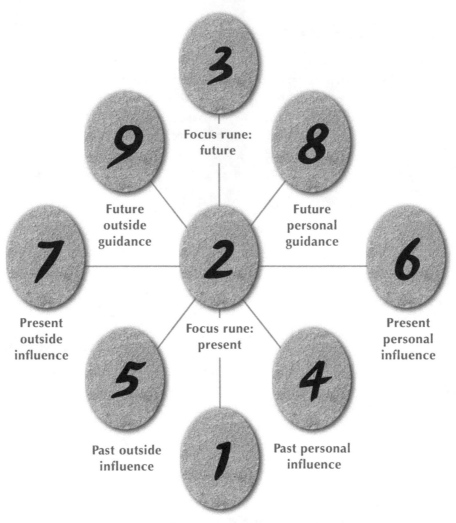

Focus rune: future

Future outside guidance

Future personal guidance

Present outside influence

Focus rune: present

Present personal influence

Past outside influence

Past personal influence

Focus rune: past

1. TIWAZ: In the recent past, Tiwaz could indicate a man as the focus, or an issue with balance, legalities, or justice.

5. LAGUZ (REVERSED): This could indicate an issue with a woman or the querent's unwillingness to go with the flow of a situation, as Laguz is a rune of water.

4. OTHALA (REVERSED): This means that there have been some issues on the home front or that there may be problems with family or extended family. It could also mean that the querent had issues with feeling "at home."

2. HAGALAZ: Having Hagalaz here may indicate that the querent is experiencing annoying obstacles. Feelings of being pummeled with problems abound. They may agree that challenges have come more often and stress is taking its toll.

7. GIFU: Gifu here shows that the querent is experiencing some sort of exchange of energy or action. They may be giving too much or not receiving enough, and a romance may be the current focus.

6. ANSUZ (REVERSED): Ansuz reversed here shows issues with communication. The querent may not be communicating well with others, or knowledge of a situation may be lacking.

3. FEHU: Fehu in the future shows that abundance will be available in the future if things go as planned. It also denotes a focus on financial stability, which is possible with the right actions.

9. MANNAZ: Mannaz in this position shows support within some sort of group situation. Look for support from mentors, counselors, friends, or organizations. These will all be influences on the querent's future.

8. ISA: Isa here asks for time for self-care. The querent can make themself available and ready to receive abundance by seeking a balance within. Isa is also symbolic of a halting of things, so it could also ask for something to stop to make the abundance happen. Regardless, self-care will be important.

LAST BUT NOT LEAST

Sometimes there still may be some unanswered questions in a rune reading or another lingering question about which you want more insight. Maybe one of the runes needs clarification. This is a good time to pick a single rune and use it to answer questions outside of the regular layout.

You will need to have another set of runes to draw from. Simply lay out the runes facedown, choose a single stave, and turn it over like a book for a forward and reversed orientation. This technique can be used when trying to gain more insight from a specific rune in the reading or as an extra question and answer regarding a related topic. This is a great way to offer a little more insight to any reading no matter what runic layout you are using. Just taking the time to do so based on your intuition may result in impactful insight.

KEY TAKEAWAYS

Understanding rune spreads takes time and study. In this chapter, you learned about a variety of rune-casting techniques and rune spreads. The layouts in this book are only a sampling of the many spreads developed by experienced rune-workers. You should also feel free to develop your own using elements from the various available rune spreads. As we get ready to move to the next chapter, remember:

◆ Casting methods include tossing and dropping a set or random numbers of runes with a specific intention.

◆ Single-rune pulls are ideal for daily runic study. Put yourself on a thirty-day program and pull a rune a day. Journal about your experience.

◆ Rune spreads are different from casting. Different layouts serve different purposes and intentions.

◆ Rune spreads can be done with a single rune or up to nine, as discussed in this chapter.

◆ Many rune spreads can offer a focused reading for a specific issue.

◆ Journal your journey and keep a record of your experiences and progress.

CHAPTER TEN

Practicing Rune Magic

FEHU

YOUR FINANCIAL FRIEND

Fehu personifies a cycle of abundance. Write Fehu on the inside of your wallet, the corners of your bills, and your bank statements, or incorporate it into your signature when you endorse checks before depositing them. If you keep a piggy bank or have a mason jar savings account, paint or write Fehu on it. Invoke Fehu every time you send money, energy, or other resources in hopes it will stimulate the economy and spread abundance wherever it goes. Remember, Fehu isn't about hoarding wealth, it's about having enough for yourself as well as others. The exchange of money can be honored by being generous and offering help when others are in need.

Create a "money pouch" by putting a Fehu rune in a cloth bag. Add a leaf of basil, a malachite stone, and a small piece of devil's shoestring root (available at health or metaphysical stores or online). Fold up a dollar bill and put it in the bag as well. Keep this bag with you when working, put it under your pillow at night to encourage insight via dreams, and have it nearby when paying bills. You can keep it wherever you want money to come in, such as a purse, wallet, or cash register.

For an effective candle ritual, carve Fehu on a chime candle three times and coat it in an oil that promotes manifestation, abundance, or attraction. Use basil, cinquefoil, and alfalfa to dress the candle. Light it and let it burn all the way down to promote a cycle of wealth and abundance.

Fehu can also be meditated with and its name chanted to offer clarity in financially stressful situations. When nothing else can be done or you are in need of a windfall, sit with Fehu and chant its name slowly. Be open to receiving even though you don't know where it will come from. Be okay with this and open to opportunity. Meditate for as long as you need to, and do this for nine days as a personal ritual to encourage manifestation.

Even when money is tight, find some way to pay it forward, even if it is simply giving a dollar to someone in need, a quarter to a child, or maybe even a larger tip than usual at your favorite restaurant. Fehu is a cyclical rune, so doing what you can personally to save what you have and negotiate spending will help Fehu bring the cycle back around to your favor. Fehu is not about wasting money or spending unwisely.

URUZ
HEALING WATERS

Uruz is known as a rune of healing and vitality. As such, its energies can be called upon for effective and powerful self-care. The mind and spirit can do amazing things when we set intentions. Just having the right mindset can greatly affect the way we heal from injury and illness. When we invoke runes for these purposes, we not only activate the energies of the runes, but we also set the intention of healing within our subconscious. There are several ways to use Uruz for healing and vitality. Here, you'll learn to create rune-charged water that offers an invigorating refreshment while promoting healing.

Fill a large glass or water bottle with filtered or moon-charged water and draw the rune Uruz on the side of the vessel with a marker or your finger. Before drinking, ask Uruz to offer vitality and healing to you as you drink it. To charge this even further, try adding a clear quartz crystal to the water and letting it sit overnight. Notice how it actually tastes different and changes your mood and energy through the day. Focus your intentions on health and vitality with each sip.

You can ritualize this practice any way you wish. Find a special vessel for your healing water. Write or trace the rune Uruz on the side of it. Add your glass of Uruz-intentioned water to your altar. Light a white or green candle and offer your favorite incense. Meditate with intentions to Freya and or Freyr to bless your waters with healing properties. Pass the vessel of water over the candle flame, then through the incense smoke while doing so. This offers representations of all the four elements: Earth, Air, Fire, and Water.

Uruz-intentioned water can be made for almost any reason. Consider it when watering plants to promote healthy leaves and root growth. Trace a quick rune over your cup when having morning coffee or tea. Add Uruz-charged water to a bath along with complementing herbs for a relaxing, healing bath.

THURISAZ
THORN BOUNDARIES

Setting boundaries can be difficult, especially for some empaths who feel the pressure of others' wants and needs to the detriment of their own health and happiness. Certain environments, such as work, public shopping, concerts, or gatherings, can be difficult, too, especially around people who may exude their own energies with greater intensity than others. They can simply walk by and one can feel a heaviness.

Sometimes those who are in need of help or care can produce energy that can take a toll on one's spirit. People in the health care industry or first responders may be prone to this sort of energy manipulation by the very people they are trying to help. Many times these folks don't even know why they are drained or on edge all the time. Their commitment to others puts them in a line of energetic fire.

Thurisaz can represent a thorn on a rosebush, protecting the beautiful flower. It also represents Thor and his mighty hammer, Mjolnir. Thor was a friend to humankind and was said to be a loyal protector. When invoking Thurisaz for protection, think of Thor protecting you. Think of how you are using this "thorn" to protect yourself and your spirit. Thurisaz is also a truly powerful rune, and when others wish you harm, it can protect you and send the intended negativity back to the sender tenfold.

To strengthen your boundary-setting abilities, wear or carry Thurisaz somewhere on your person. Many wear a hammer pendant for this, as Thor was known to shrink down his hammer and wear it on a chain around his neck so as not to intimidate his human friends. Use this symbol as your armor, imagining a protective barrier of energy all around you.

Another way to represent Thurisaz for protection is to inscribe it on both sides of an actual thorn of a rosebush. Put the thorn into a small container or pouch and carry it with you. One can also hang this or any other Thurisaz-inspired talisman or charm above the front door of a home to keep it protected from theft or weather.

Part of this boundary-setting process includes taking the time not only to protect yourself, but to ground and cleanse afterward. "Protect, ground, and cleanse" should be the spiritual trinity you use to stay protected on a consistent basis.

ANSUZ
A RITUAL FOR CLARITY

Words have power. Not just in magic, but in everything we think and do. Words wield intentions and energy to others as well as ourselves. One can invoke the powers of Ansuz to foster better communication with others and change negative self-talk into positive affirmations.

To bring clarity to a situation or when communication is failing in some respect, try working an altar for Odin using Ansuz as the focus. Odin is known as the god of knowledge and wisdom. His quest for insight was the focus of many of his adventures. Ansuz is associated with Odin and one can invoke the powers of communication through an altar ritual for the chief Norse god.

To set up the altar, bring in a runestave (letter symbol) of Ansuz and use it as the centerpiece or focus of the altar. Next, find a representation of Odin and place it in the northern part of the altar. You'll need a bay leaf and writing utensil, as well as something to burn the bay leaf in. When you are ready, you can begin the ritual.

1. Light three candles for the Norns (the sisters of past, present, and future) and offer incense.

2. Make an offering of clear water in a glass bowl or cup. This water represents the well of Mimir, the source of wisdom Odin gave his eye to drink from. You can place a clear quartz in the vessel of water as well to charge it with energy. This crystal represents Odin's sacrificed eye.

3. Sit and meditate with the rune Ansuz. Trace it with your finger and envision Odin's ravens, Hugin and Munin, flying across the realms. Put yourself in a state where you can see higher perspectives. Be open to receiving messages and focus on relieving yourself of any negative self-talk.

4. Chant the word "Ansuz" nine times. Focus on the energy around your throat and picture it becoming a clear ball of light.

5. After a few moments, take the bay leaf and write the rune Ansuz on it. On the other side, write the word "Ansuz" and then light it from one of the candles. Let it burn in a firesafe vessel, and while it does, make intentions for a stronger sense of personal communication and clarity in understanding others' perspectives.

When the ritual is complete, thank the gods and all those watching over you. You can keep the altar set up for three days (or as long as needed) and repeat the ritual if you're feeling called to it.

RAIDHO

THE TRAVELER'S RUNE

Traveling is always an adventure. Whether you're taking a flight, road trip, or ocean cruise, getting to your intended destination smoothly can sometimes be problematic. Many trips are pleasant getaways and many daily drives are uneventful, but sometimes a little rune magic can keep trips smooth and obstacles to a minimum.

Raidho is an ideal rune to use when traveling. It should be considered as important as packing your bags and being on time for a flight. Raidho offers energies of protection, adventure, inspiration, and enjoyment of the journey. With the right intentions, it can make a potentially stressful trip a more rewarding experience for all involved.

When traveling by air, there are a few ways to use Raidho. The airport can be a chaotic place filled with people and all their energies. Tensions can be high, and when issues occur, energies all around can be rife with negativity, anger, and irritations. Raidho can help you navigate these energies and flow through them with few challenges. Carry the Raidho rune with you on your journey. Write the rune Raidho on your luggage with the intention that it all reaches its proper destination. Use Raidho as a mental mantra when waiting in line, checking baggage, or working through flight details.

If a road trip is planned, Raidho can be used in much the same way. Place the rune Raidho in the vehicle as a talisman for safety and pleasant travels. Trace it on the dashboard to help avoid any roadside situations. Draw Raidho on bags or luggage. One can even draw Raidho on the tires of a vehicle when going on long journeys across the country.

If enjoying a journey on the sea, Raidho can be paired with Laguz with intentions to the Norse god Njord, the god of the sea. If on a lake, Laguz can also represent Freya, the goddess of love, beauty, and sorcery, who will help you have a safe and pleasant time on her waters.

You can also make a bindrune talisman for any trip using a combination of runes with Raidho as the focus. Consider Tiwaz, Thurisaz, Ansuz, Algiz, and Kenaz for other runes to combine with Raidho. Create the bindrune sigil and carve it on a piece of wood or other material and carry it with you on your travels.

KENAZ
A RUNE GRID FOR CREATIVITY

Kenaz is a wonderful rune to use when wanting to find your inspiration. It represents the light in the darkness, the torch in the tunnel. It is the fire of inspiration artists use to create. If you are a creative sort, this rune can be a trusted companion. Artists are typically their own worst critics, and keeping the inspirations coming can be challenging at times.

Use Kenaz in a crystal grid to help generate a field of inspirational energy. Crystals can be tapped and activated on a grid to provide a powerful tool for use in creative endeavors. Runes are much like crystals, as they can be charged with intention and used in a grid that channels their energies and links them to the stones alongside them.

To make a rune grid for Kenaz that inspires creativity, you will need the following:

◆ A small piece of paper with the rune Kenaz inscribed on it

◆ A soft cloth on which to set up the grid (six to twelve inches is fine) or use a standard sacred geometry rune grid

◆ A quartz point crystal for the center of the grid. Size doesn't matter here. This can also be a simple polished and tumbled quartz.

◆ Three amethyst stones. Points or tumbled and polished work well.

◆ Three citrine stones. Raw or polished and tumbled are fine for this. You can also substitute other stones for creativity here, such as pyrite, sodalite, ouro verde quartz, or aventurine.

◆ A wand. This can be another quartz point, wood wand, or even your finger.

To set up the grid, first place the paper with the rune Kenaz inscribed on it in the center of the cloth. Next, place the quartz point on top of the paper. This is what is known as the "engine" of the grid. Place the three amethyst stones around the engine in a triangular pattern. Place the citrine stones in the same manner with an opposing triangular pattern. You should now have the six stones surrounding the engine.

To activate the grid, take your wand (or finger) and start at the engine. Draw an imaginary line from the engine to the first stone and back again. Repeat this process with each stone. Imagine connecting each stone to the engine with the intentional energies of your wand. When you come back around to the engine, make a swirling motion upward, funneling the energy throughout the room, creating a field of inspiration.

GIFU

FOR BALANCE, BLISS, AND BONDING

Gifu is a fantastic rune for anything that has to do with partnership, love, romance, lust, giving, and receiving. It's a very balanced rune that also signifies a bond or mutual friendship. Gifu can be used in many ways to facilitate lasting friendships, true love, self-love, and even lust-filled flings. It is the embodiment of a win-win attitude.

Below are some methods to use when wanting to invoke the energies of Gifu into your life. Remember, when performing any work with Gifu, make balance the focus of the intentions. The win-win spirit will leave all parties satisfied and yearning for more in the future.

- The symbol of Gifu can be signified in a handfasting ceremony—a ritual in which a couple's hands are tied together to symbolize bonding with another. The cord or cloth used in tying the hands together is crossed in an X, representing the bond the couple has. A simple ceremony can be held with a partner to signify an exclusive relationship, marriage, or lasting bond of trust.

- Baking is a language of love, and one can make biscuits or small cakes with an X marked on the top, signifying Gifu. Make these on special occasions for meals celebrating family, friends, and lovers. Add poppy seeds to promote love, as well as calming rest when the excitement is over.

- Carrying Gifu with you or written on you will open up a path of mutual exchange throughout the day. You will notice the rune Gifu in nature and in your surroundings. Hold this rune in your hand to facilitate a feeling of calming balance. Imbue it with intentions of a win-win spirit and journal about your experiences with it.

- Carve Gifu on a red chime candle and coat it with clove oil, using cinnamon and mullein to dress it. Burn this candle for or during romantic encounters with intentions of love, lust, and mutual satisfaction.

- Use Gifu as a focus for meditation when working to dispel any negative self-talk. Sometimes we have trouble taking a simple compliment without negating it with internal sarcasm. Gifu can help with acceptance and receiving from others without guilt or self-judgment. Create a bindrune or a charm with Gifu and take it out often to remind yourself to enjoy acceptance from others without feeling like you have to give too much in return. Use it as a tool for balance as you maneuver through your day.

WUNJO
CANDLE MAGIC FOR JOY AND VICTORY

Candle rituals are a great way to invoke runes for a specific purpose. These ceremonies are simple and fun to perform, offering an experience for all the senses. They also set intentions deeply into the mind and spirit. Candle rituals call upon the energies of our guides, guardians, and gods to influence our lives through our higher selves to help us achieve our goals and gain inspiration.

Wunjo is a rune of victory and joy. When in a state of depression or unease, this rune can help inspire a change in your attitude. If you are working on a project or going through a challenging experience, call on Wunjo to help see things through to a victorious end. You might be so involved in a project that answers to challenges can go unseen. A candle ritual using Wunjo can offer joy in the process and bring clarity to the challenges. Use the following as a guide to perform your own candle ritual for success and victory.

For this ritual, you will need a white or orange chime candle, an oil for dressing the candle (crown of success or similar), something with which to inscribe the candle (e.g., thumbtack, old ballpoint pen, bone candle pick), and any of the following herbs: cinnamon, cinquefoil, clover, ginger, or High John the Conqueror.

Inscribe the candle with Wunjo three or nine times (both are sacred numbers). You can also use Wunjo in a bindrune with other runes and inscribe that to the side of the candle once. Grind your herbs with intention, and pour out the resulting powder onto a sheet of paper. Add some of the oil to your fingers and/or to the candle itself. Dress the candle with the oil, with a motion going from the wick to the base. Roll the candle gently in the herb mixture, coating it in its entirety. Place the candle in a holder and then onto your altar.

On a piece of paper, write out your intentions. This could be just to inspire joy, overcome a challenge, or achieve victory in some way. Make it simple. Fold the paper three times and place it under the candleholder. Light the candle and let it burn all the way down. When it has fully burned out, take the paper and burn it in a firesafe place or receptacle. Let the intentions flow out into the universe and call upon Tyr to bring you victory.

Chime candles are inexpensive and last around thirty minutes. Feel free to add any other ritual intentions, crystals, or anything else to this ceremony.

HAGALAZ
RITUALS FOR HABITUALS

Hagalaz is a fantastic rune for quick changes and transformation, such as letting go of habits or routines hindering your growth. These changes can be permanent or temporary, depending on the habit. For example, you may need to quit drinking, as alcoholism has taken hold. This would require a permanent transformation. On the other hand, a woman may need to quit drinking only during her pregnancy for the health of the baby.

When going through change, call upon Hagalaz in rituals to offer support. These rituals can be used to ease or eliminate unhealthy habits, change up routines, alter mindsets, and offer the confidence to navigate changes.

To "freeze" a bad habit or practice, create a Hagalaz-infused freezer spell. Find a small but freezer-safe vessel. On a piece of paper, write out the result you wish to experience. Feel free to add a totem of any sort that represents the habit into the vessel (e.g., a cigarette butt for smoking cessation, a dollar bill for overspending, a piece of food for unhealthy eating, a pill for drug use). Fold the paper with the intention three times and place it into the vessel. Fill the vessel with filtered or moon water, leaving room for expansion during freezing. Add a pinch of salt to help eliminate negativity. Seal the vessel and wrap it in tin foil with the shiny side facing inward. Inscribe Hagalaz on the top of the vessel with a permanent marker. Place it in the freezer and keep it there for as long as needed. If you feel it's no longer needed, toss in the trash or bury it.

Another way for Hagalaz to offer support during challenging times is to make a worry-stone talisman. Simply find a stone that feels good in your hand. Adorn the stone with the rune Hagalaz using white paint. Carry this stone with you or have it nearby when fighting off addictive tendencies.

Perform a candle ritual like the one described for Wunjo to help overcome addiction or routine. Inscribe a white candle with Hagalaz three times and dress with an oil that feels appropriate for this application to you. Use any combination of the following herbs: catnip, cayenne, damiana, mugwort, mullein, passionflower, and Saint-John's-wort. Write the intention or your desired outcome on a bay leaf and burn it using the candle flame.

NAUTHIZ
CREATING A NEED-FIRE

Nauthiz represents our basic human needs. If you are in survival mode or struggling for what seems to be longer than necessary, you may feel unsure of your future stability and may need to prepare for upcoming challenges. Nauthiz can be invoked for help meeting your basic needs, such as for food, shelter, warmth, power, and transportation.

A rune-worker can create a need-fire using an altar cauldron, campfire, or firepit. For a cauldron ritual, use a small piece of paper or a bay leaf. Inscribe your needs. If using paper, fold it three times and inscribe "Nauthiz" on the outside. If using a bay leaf, write "Nauthiz" on the backside. Light a brown, green, white, or yellow chime candle, as well as your favorite incense. Run the paper or leaf over the candle flame, asking Freya to bless it. Run it then through the smoke of the incense, asking Freyr to honor it. Burn the intention in the cauldron.

If using a firepit or outdoor campfire, feel free to use a larger piece of paper and write out your needs in more detail. When you're done, fold the paper three times and write "Nauthiz" on it. Offer this to the fire. You can also offer a totem in ritual sacrifice if it feels applicable for the need. For example, if you're in need of transportation or housing, draw a car or house on the dollar bill as well as the rune Nauthiz and offer it to the fire. Unfortunately, money is one of the biggest needs we face daily. Some have too much, and others have very little. Sacrificing a dollar bill (or a representation of one) or other personal item, such as food or a totem, to the fire is a way to surrender to the universe and be open to unexpected windfalls.

Be clear in the difference between your needs and your wants. Nauthiz is a balanced rune, and balance is the key to survival. Rituals with Nauthiz as the focus rune help you see what your needs truly are. When those are met, your wants can be manifested without sacrificing your needs, thereby offering greater balance in life.

ISA
A FORTRESS OF SOLITUDE MEDITATION

Isa is a fantastic rune for meditation. The following is a quick meditation you can use to access peace and insight. Use it as the basis for extended meditations if doing shadow work, chakra alignment, astral projection, or sleep meditation. Have someone read it aloud to you or record it yourself for use in meditation. Modify it as you see fit.

Lay down and relax in a comfortable position. Let the concerns of the day and thoughts of the future all drift away. Breathe deeply in and focus all your stresses into one compact thought. Then transform those thoughts into love energy, and breathe out nothing but love. Do this three times. In with the stress, out with the love.

Now picture yourself in the middle of an icicle. You are safe and protected by a thick wall of ice. There are no distractions here—no phones, no computers, and no people or jobs—just you, calm and relaxed. This is your fortress of solitude, your sacred sanctuary, a place of peace and truth.

Visualize the rune Isa, a straight line of white energy, spanning from the top of your head to your toes. It runs through all your chakras and energy centers, energizing each. Now picture a ring of white light running over you. As it passes over your face, it relaxes every muscle. As it drifts around your neck, it calms your throat and shoulders. As it passes over your chest, it calms your breathing and slows your heart rate. As it moves to your hips, it relieves the stress in your lower back and pelvis. As it follows your legs, every muscle relaxes comfortably. As it passes over your calves, they release any stress. And as it passes over your feet, all stress and tension dissipate into the universe. You are calm, safe, open, and at ease. Take a deep breath and hold it for three seconds. Release it slowly while saying "Isa" in a long, whispering manner. Do this three times.

Visualize yourself now, embraced in light inside your icicle. All concerns are outside, while inside, you are relaxed and bathed in a healing light. With each breath, you grow more relaxed. With each breath, you sink deeper down, releasing any tension into the ether.

Love is the most powerful energy in the universe, so take it with you to give you strength and compassion as you fall even deeper into a state of blissful relaxation. From here, you can travel without moving. Your mind is ready to journey within.

JERA
GROWING THINGS

Jera represents harvest, cycles, and seasons. To connect with Jera, experience the life cycle of a plant from seedling to harvest firsthand. You can plant seeds yourself or purchase a young plant for your home. Herbs for your kitchen are rewarding and fairly easy, and many people enjoy eating the plants they grow. Herbs are also important in various magical practices, and the intentions you put into them by growing them yourself makes them all the more effective. Pick something you'll use often and enjoy the cycle of Jera in its growth.

Mark Jera on the surface of the soil near the base of your plant by scratching it with a stick, arranging sticks or stones, or placing a charged talisman bearing Jera on the soil. As you care for the plant, periodically recharge the rune at its base. As you do so, chant the word "Jera" repeatedly as if speaking to the plant. Give the plants you grow special attention. Call upon Freyr, the god of the harvest, to see your plant friends and help them thrive.

Some stones are also known to help with plant growth. Kambaba jasper, moss agate, and tree agate all work well to promote growth. Place these stones in the pot or at the base of the plant. If you like, inscribe or draw Jera on them to add even more intentions. You can also take a clear quartz crystal and place it in a vessel of water. Leave this overnight and use it to water your plants. This charged water will add more intentional energies to your herbs, enhancing the powers of any other stones you use as well.

If you want to work more spellwork into your magic micro-garden, you can plant your intentions in the soil beneath your plant so your daily plant care becomes a long-term spell rather than a meditative practice. Bury a charged sigil, runescript, bindrune, or other talisman or meaningful object in the soil near the base of the container. Transplant your seedling directly over the buried talisman or spell paper. Tuck it in with soil and water and follow the same instructions described above.

EIHWAZ
LETTING IT GO

Sometimes you have to let things go to make room for growth. These can be physical things or aspects of yourself that hold you back. Letting go can be freeing. It can transform your life. But you must be willing and able to fully embrace the release.

Do you remember the fun of tossing a stone into a body of water? Whether trying to get the most skips or the biggest splash, sending a rock to a watery grave was always satisfying and oddly cathartic. As humans, our ties to water are all encompassing. The rune of Eihwaz is associated with the Norse goddess Freya, daughter to the sea god Njord, who is associated with the rune Laguz. Looking at this rune, it looks like two Laguz runes strung end to end.

The mysteries of the sea and other bodies of water have always fascinated humans, and many secrets have been offered to their depths. Seafarers surrendered their dead to the sea, survivors sent messages in a bottle, and many civilizations had sacred ceremonies involving water. The following is a ritual you can perform to foster the release of things that no longer serve you, using water as your conduit.

This ritual can be done with any body of water. If using a river or lake, call to Freya to bless the ritual. If using the ocean, ask Njord to honor your magical efforts. First, find three palm-sized stones. Sandstones or river rock are fine. With a permanent marker, write the following on the first stone: "I release my fears." On the second, write: "I release all judgment." On the third stone, write whatever else you intend to release. On the other side of each rock, write the rune Eihwaz.

Find a body of water where you can relax and focus undistracted. Create a sacred space by asking the nature spirits and your own guides to be there with you. Take a moment to meditate with the stones, reading each one and putting your intention and truth into them. Focus on letting go of whatever is holding you back. Releasing trauma, anguish, ego, and fear.

Take the rocks and one by one, throw them into the body of water, calling to either Freya or Njord as you do so. As you throw the rocks, allow the energy that no longer serves you to go with them to the bottom of the water. Give a battle cry for extra energy if you feel so inclined.

PERTHO
ROLLING WITH ADVANTAGE

Any pouch, box, cup, or other vessel that contains a set of runes is essentially the material manifestation of Pertho. After all, you never know what may come out of it! Pertho represents mystery, chance, and all the aspects of luck. It can promote luck in gambling or games of chance. It can offer energies that allow for things to happen unexpectedly, windfalls or otherwise. When things are out of our hands and the only thing left is a chance to roll the dice on a situation, Pertho can let us roll with advantage.

To make a Pertho gambler's potion, you will need these ingredients:

Small jar of whiskey (¾ full)
Few small pieces devil's shoestring root
¼ teaspoon camphor
Small piece of pyrite

When you are ready, follow these steps.

1. Fill a small jar three-quarters full of any whiskey (don't worry, even if you imbibe, you won't be drinking this).

2. Add a few small pieces of devil's shoestring root. Add ¼ teaspoon of camphor and a splash of water to top it off. Top with a small piece of pyrite and put the lid on.

3. Draw the rune Pertho on the side of the jar.

4. Place the jar on your altar and light three candles, one for each of the Norns, and perform a small ritual to add your intentions.

Before gambling or engaging in games of chance, you can dab a few drops of this potion into your hands and rub them together, chanting Pertho as you do so. This should help increase your luck and enhance your strategy in games.

Rituals and ceremonies with Pertho as the focus can also help offer intentions of increased luck, especially during times when you're feeling particularly unlucky in life. Spending time with Pertho may show you that you are luckier than you know. Use Pertho in ceremonies or meditation to help you start to notice your luck. You may start to find "lucky pennies" on the ground or come across a four-leaf clover. You might find your luck is avoiding trouble or illness but not necessarily winning the lottery. Using Pertho in rituals can help open your eyes to see more clearly the luck you truly have within.

ALGIZ
POWERFUL PROTECTION POWDER

Sometimes negative energies or entities linger in our home or environment. Negative energies can be brought in simply through others' spiritual baggage or attachments. Entities can cause and/or feed off depression, anger, stress, and anxiety. Those that are spiritually gifted, empathic, or energetically connected may experience these energies more easily than others. Children are especially prone to experiencing entities, apparitions, and other mysteries from beyond the veil that separates our world from the other.

Algiz is associated with the Norse god Heimdall, who guarded the Rainbow Bridge that connected Asgard with the other realms. He saw all and was prepared to defend against any foe. Call upon these aspects of Heimdall while creating a powerful protection powder that will help thicken the veil and offer protection against negative people, environments, or entities that may come into your life.

To make this powder you will need:

Crushed selenite
Crushed carborundum
Crushed black tourmaline
A spoonful of black salt
A small leaf of dried white sage

Proportions will not matter much here depending on what you can find. Just use small amounts of each ingredient and modify to fit your vessel. You can find the stones at most rock or metaphysical stores.

Selenite is a cleansing stone that can clear negative energies. Carborundum is a form of slag that has a rainbow of colors in its black material. This stone helps clear negative entities and energies. Black salt is protective and used in many banishment rituals.

When you are ready, follow the steps on the next page to create the powder.

1. Simply crush up the stones (each is soft, so crushing should be easy) until you have about a tablespoon of each.

2. Then add the black salt.

3. Find a small glass jar with a lid and fill it with the rock and salt mix.

4. Add a small piece of dried white sage as a protective blessing. Cap it with the lid.

5. You can now seal it by drawing the rune Algiz on the lid and performing a small creation ceremony with it on your altar. Ask Heimdall to see the powder and imbue it with protective properties.

Use a small portion of this powder for protection. You can sprinkle it across thresholds, on windowsills, or under a bed to ward off negative energy and unwanted spiritual visitors. It can be put into a pouch and hung above a doorway as well.

If a child is having nightmares, place this powder in a bag and under their pillow to fend off bad dreams. Add a K2 jasper stone along with it to quell night terrors.

SOWILO
SUN TEA

Take advantage of the next sunny day to make a batch of supercharged Sowilo sun tea. Unlike standard sun tea, Sowilo tea not only uses the life-giving power of the sun, which Sowilo represents, but it also incorporates your own intentions to bring joyful, energetic properties to your beverage. Making Sowilo tea is easy and can help you celebrate a bright, sunny afternoon even when life is keeping you indoors.

To create your Sowilo tea, first fill a clear glass bottle or sun tea jug with clean spring water and the tea or herbs you want to infuse it with. Sun tea brews weaker than tea made with boiling water, so use two to three times the tea you normally would. For a single serving, use three tea bags, or fifteen grams, of tea, but adjust to taste. Black tea (aka red tea or hong cha) makes a great sun tea. Saint-John's-wort and yellow chrysanthemum are great herbal choices for caffeine-free solar infusions.

In red, mark Sowilo one or more times on the outside of the bottle. Once you have added the tea and herbs you wish to use, place the bottle outdoors in full sun and let it steep a full twenty-four hours. Feel free to add a clear quartz crystal for an extra boost. The next day, strain out the solids and enjoy.

For the most authentic bottled sunlight experience, imbibe immediately outdoors. As you drink it, soak up some sunlight and appreciate the warmth of Sowilo as it flows through your body. This tea can be used to help bring inspiration to your day or at least a moment of joy to appreciate. Each time you drink it, imagine it acting as a magical potion that changes your attitude and emotions. With each sip, make intentions for your body to awaken and thrive.

TIWAZ
SMELLS LIKE JUSTICE

The following is a recipe for Tyr's victory powder, an incense that can be used to create success in legal matters. Tyr's powder is a blend of herbs and incense that you can burn for rituals or before legal proceedings. You can pass legal notices through its smoke for intentions of victory. This powder can also be used in candle rituals for courtroom success. To make this recipe, you'll need a mortar and pestle, as well as a glass bowl and a vessel in which to put the powder.

For this recipe you will need:

1 tablespoon sandalwood incense or 1 teaspoon powdered sandalwood incense
1 tablespoon myrrh incense or 1 teaspoon powdered myrrh incense
2 drops court case oil
⅛ ounce dried white sage (loose)
⅛ ounce dried calendula
⅛ ounce dried deer's tongue
Pinch of flat cedar

1. Grind the incense. This can be done in the mortar and pestle or in an old coffee grinder. Two cones of each should suffice. If using prepowdered incense, use one teaspoon of each. Pour the powdered incense mixture into a glass bowl and set it aside.

2. Grind up equal amounts of the white sage, calendula, and deer's tongue in the mortar and pestle. Add a pinch of the flat cedar and grind it into a powder.

3. Combine the ground incense and the herbal mix together and add the court case oil. Mix it well. Adjust the amounts as you are intuitively called to.

4. Pour the mixture into a cleansed vessel for storage. Add the Tiwaz rune on the vessel as a blessing. Burn a small amount of this mixture on top of self-lighting charcoal (the kind used for hookahs) for victorious intentions, or use the powder to dress candles in rituals for success in all legal matters.

BERKANA
BERKANA BREW

Where birch trees grow, you will often find chaga, a cold-climate parasitic fungus sometimes known as King of the Mushrooms. Chaga supports physical health and immune function in a number of ways and contains compounds with antioxidant, anti-inflammatory, and anticarcinogenic properties.

You can take chaga internally as a tea or tincture or apply it topically in the form of an oil or salve. It is available in many forms, including capsules, powder, premade tea, chaga butter, hot chocolate, and chaga soup. These can all be found in health stores or online.

If you require a higher dose of healing Berkana energy and are ready to level up your self-care routine, make some space in your home for a slow cooker where you can always have chaga brewing. Purchase lumps of chaga and wrap about one ounce in cheesecloth and kitchen twine or place it in a muslin bag. Fill the slow cooker with clean spring water, add the chaga, and leave it to simmer overnight.

When you first brew it, the chaga broth should be rich and dark and taste earthy. You may like it plain or with honey and cinnamon, or you can mask the flavor but keep the benefits by using it to brew your favorite tea or pour-over coffee. Alternatively, you can chill batches of chaga and enjoy it plain or mixed with cold-brew coffee. Each time you take from your chaga pot, add more water and let it continue brewing. After a few weeks, the liquid will become very diluted. At this point, replace your chaga chunks and use the old ones in a foot soak, give them to the garden, or dry them out and use them to make a tincture.

However you use chaga, incorporate aspects of Berkana into it. Use intentions of new beginnings, fresh starts, new ideas, or maternal instincts. When drinking it, be sure to think of how it will help heal and refresh your body, protect you from illness, and fill you with inspiring ideas. Doing this is a form of positive self-talk and triggers your subconscious to take action within your body.

EHWAZ
LOVE LETTERS

Ehwaz is a rune of partnerships. A rune that represents the bond between two people who are close enough to know each other inside and out. Like the connection between a horse and rider, this bond sometimes shines even when no words are spoken. Ehwaz represents mutual support and trust between the two parties.

How is the bond represented by Ehwaz manifested in your life? Do you have a partner with whom you have an ineffable mutual bond? If so, write them a love letter of appreciation. Thank them for their support and tell them how much you appreciate what they bring to your life. Don't worry, you won't have to give this letter to the person if you don't want to. Writing these things down by hand offers a personal experience that teaches us to take the time to appreciate and be grateful.

When you are done, sign Ehwaz near your name and charge it (after all, this rune is a sort of love letter in itself). Afterward, give the other person the letter if you are so inclined. Otherwise you can keep the letter for another time, or ritually burn it and send the intentions into the universe. You can also write to someone you're still manifesting, and if you take that route, burn the letter to send it off and let the universe know what sort of partnership you're ready for.

This exercise may help you appreciate those close to you more deeply. It may inspire you to actually buy that birthday card or pick up flowers for a loved one. When we sit down and list out all the things we appreciate in a partner, we start to see through the mundane. Physically showing ourselves how we appreciate someone can recharge stagnant feelings in a relationship.

Another take on this process is to write a love letter to yourself. Take time to sit and write a letter stating all the things you appreciate about yourself. Mention all your strengths and inspirations. Thank yourself for putting in the work to make a better you. Tell yourself how much you appreciate various aspects of your personality. If you feel like writing something negative or self-deprecating, stop and rewind. Only write as if you were writing to your lover. Write like you are lifting someone up with the kind of support only Ehwaz can represent.

MANNAZ
RUNIC SUPPORT SYSTEM

Mannaz is the rune of humankind. It represents the support of a group of people and is ideal for use at work. Sometimes a work situation lacks the support of its team. Problems with coworker personalities can create tension and conflict in a work environment. For some, work can be mundane and lacking in any sort of personal fulfillment. Obstacles in career advancement can lead to depression and financial stress.

◆ To foster a good work environment, a team mentality, or support in a collaboration, one can use the support system of Mannaz.

◆ For help in finding a new job, invoke Mannaz when filling out the application. If it is a paper application, write Mannaz somewhere on it in a small and subtle rune. If it is an online application, trace Mannaz on the computer screen over the finished application before attaching it to a response email.

◆ When working with others on a project or collaboration, write Mannaz on a piece of paper and fold it three times. Keep it in your pocket or with your things while attending meetings.

◆ To help keep a frustrating coworker at bay, create a talisman using Mannaz, Thurisaz, and Algiz. Combine the runes into a bindrune and inscribe it on a suitable material. This bindrune can even be written on something that is already at your desk in view of the offending coworker. Take the talisman and wear it, carry it, or place it between you and the other person. Use a black tourmaline stone at your desk to offer psychic protection and grounding.

◆ Perform a candle ritual the night before making any presentation. Inscribe Mannaz on a chime candle and coat it with Employment oil (or any other suitable oil). Dress the candle in cinquefoil. Write down your intentions on a piece of paper and fold it three times. Set it under the base of the candleholder. Burn the candle with intentions of positive reception of your presentation.

◆ Create a sort of "work talisman" to carry with you daily. Find a Mannaz rune you can keep as a charm. This can be stone (howlite is great), wood, or any other material you find attractive. Carry this rune on you every day, and each time you put it in your pocket, make the intention to have a smooth and productive day at work. Use it to remind you to find satisfaction in whatever you can throughout the day. Let it be a charm of making that brings energies of support and teamwork to your career.

LAGUZ
ELEMENTAL POWER

There are several crystals and stones that offer water energies and blend well with Laguz intentions. The following is a list of five stones and crystals with brief descriptions. Each has an energy that can help when invoking Laguz in meditations and crystal work.

AQUAMARINE: This stone is great for soothing relaxation, much like taking a refreshing shower or warm bath. It can calm and put you in touch with your higher self. Aquamarine helps dispel emotional numbness and communicate your true feelings. It can cool anger, activate the throat chakra, and clear communication.

BLUE LACE AGATE: This stone is ideal for helping you develop your intuition and communication skills. It can help you speak in public with confidence. It's also good for issues where compassion and forgiveness are needed. This is a great stone for artists, musicians, poets, teachers, caregivers, and actors.

MOLDAVITE AND TEKTITES: Tektites are created from the impact of a meteor hitting the Earth. This energy makes tektites rare and powerful. Some include Libyan desert glass and moldavite. Tektites of this sort have intense energies and are ideal for use with other stones and crystals. They can be considered a "condiment" of sorts that enhance the properties of other stones. Tektites can help you let go of things that don't serve you, bring luck and prosperity, or add powerful insight during meditation.

MOONSTONE: Filled with powerful moon energy, moonstone is perfect for enhancing female energies. Moonstone can help with pregnancy as well as postpartum recovery. It can offer a calming peace, like a mother to a child. Moonstone also enhances insight and intuition.

RUTILATED QUARTZ: This form of quartz offers intense grounding for a "go with the flow" attitude. It can stimulate your intuition and alert you when a "vibe" is off with someone or a situation. It can also be used to enhance the energies of other stones and can offer spiritual inspiration. It's ideal for bracelets or pendants.

INGWAZ
SOWING THE SEEDS OF SUCCESS

Ingwaz is a powerful rune of growth. It is the seed that was planted that is now starting to sprout. Seeds in general are often used in magical works as they contain the ingredients for life. They represent the generational cycle that carries on season after season. Seeds can lay dormant until they have just the right conditions for growth. When they do, they have the botanical blueprints they need for the specific plant they are to propagate. They push up from the soil and reach for the sun. Then they transform and grow as part of an ongoing cycle of life. Part of this cycle is to create new seeds to send out. These can be carried by the wind or by insects and animals or transmitted through feces that fertilize them wherever they are left.

Seeds can be incorporated in magical works alongside Ingwaz. Each seed has the properties of the entire plant, so they can be used to promote those herbal energies. Small seeds can be used in food, and larger seeds can be used as talismans for growth or protection. Seeds can be sprinkled on thresholds or added to magical pouches. They can be planted with intention and nurtured to bring about the desired outcome.

To bring prosperity to a home, set up a bird feeder in your yard and fill it with quality birdseed. Decorate the house with the rune Ingwaz and watch as the seeds that fall grow from the grass below. By doing this simple thing, you are engaging in a cycle of growth that promotes positivity in your personal environment. Doing it with intention further solidifies this in your mind each time you see a bird enjoy a quick meal.

There are a wide variety of seeds as well as seedpods that can be commonly found in nature. Seedpods can be used with Ingwaz and can represent the protection of the pod around the seed. Inscribe Ingwaz on a suitable flat, dried pod to create a talisman of new growth. Place it over a home-office doorway, above a window in a child's room, or over your front door.

Flowers and plants are also good representations of Ingwaz. Having flowers around the home offers a pleasant view, and their seeds can be saved and dried. You can create a special vase adorned with Ingwaz and put in flowers that represent a specific intention. When they die, bury them or use the remains as mulch. Pour out any water left in the vase over your other plants in the home to signify the cycle and sacrifice of the flowers.

DAGAZ
A TALISMAN FOR TRANSFORMATION

As the "dawn rune," Dagaz offers energies of transformation, renewal, new beginnings, and forward movement. You can create a talisman using Dagaz to assist you in your journey of self-discovery. A talisman is a personal artifact made to invoke the energies of the rune of focus. It is a sacred object, a living entity, and a trusted friend.

To make a Dagaz talisman, choose a suitable material. Options include wood, stone, oven-baked clay, a horn, or shell. Just make sure the piece can fit into your palm for easy carrying or that would serve well as a pendant for daily wear.

First, set the stage. Create a sacred workspace somewhere with no distractions. Prepare your material, giving it the shape and size you want. Then carve, paint, or draw the rune Dagaz on the intended talisman. Add your name to it and any symbol or word that represents its purpose. Finish it off in any manner you like using what seems right to you.

Next, take the intended talisman and wrap it in a cloth. Take a red cord and wrap it around the cloth nine times. Prepare your altar with candles, sage, and incense. Set a bowl, cauldron, or other vessel in the center of your altar. Hold the intended talisman in both hands and ask your guides, guardians, and Odin to bring life to this artifact. Make any offerings you wish.

Place the intended talisman in the center of the altar and let it sit overnight. In the morning, tap the package three times with a wand to wake it up. Pick it up with both hands and breathe onto it, giving it life, speaking the word "Dagaz" as you do it. Unwrap the package. You now have a living artifact that is charged with your own intentions and personal power. Wear it or carry it with you. Once the issue is resolved or the talisman is no longer required, you may keep it by offering it a sacred home on your altar or in your study, or you can ritually burn it as a sacrifice of thanks to the gods.

OTHALA
HOUSE CLEANING AND HOME BLESSING

Othala relates to aspects of the home, protection, and ancestral roots, so it's an ideal rune to use when a home needs a cleansing and blessing ceremony. Sometimes an environment can get filled with stagnant energy or arguments may have left an unpleasant vibe. A cleansing can be performed when moving into a new place to clear the previous occupants' energy and bring in your own. Cleansing can eliminate negative energy in a space and thicken the veil if entities are interfering with daily life.

Cleansings and blessings can be done easily and can provide a peaceful, calming vibe that can be physically felt when successful. To cleanse a new or existing home, the first step is to clean the home as best as possible. Remove clutter, dust, do the dishes, wash windows, and set the stage for a happy home you wish to live in.

Once the cleaning is done to your satisfaction, it is time to perform the cleansing. To do this, one can burn sage or use a sage spray. Sage clears the environment of all energy, positive and negative, providing a clean slate to bring in good energy. Open the windows and front door if possible and light a single white candle for protection.

Whether using the spray or the smoke, work your way around the home. If the home has more than one story, start downstairs and work your way up, then back down again, making sure to address every dark corner and closet. As you smoke or spritz through the house, offer intentions of positivity, cleansing, and releasing of any negative energies. If you have someone assisting you, have them play a drum or shake a rattle alongside you. This will disperse negative energy as you sage.

When you have finished, set aside the sage and burn incense to bring back positive energy into your home. You can also cook food, play music, sing, dance, or all of the above. The point is to bring back joyful energy that will embed into the foundations of your home.

Use Othala to bless your home by creating a talisman and placing it above the front door on the inside. You can inscribe Othala on the outside of the door to provide protection as well. To bless the remainder of the home, you can trace Othala on (or in the air in front of) every window of the home. This will offer ancestral protection and bless your home with your own good vibrations and positive intentions.

A FINAL NOTE

Thank you, dear reader, for taking the time to purchase this book and add it to your library of runic resources. I hope the reading experience resonated with you and that it inspires you to continue learning about runes, as well as the great history of the Norse and Germanic peoples.

As you digest all the runic lore and techniques, you will find your own path. Don't doubt yourself or worry that you might do something wrong. You won't anger the gods by practicing your craft however feels right for you. In fact, they may reveal themselves during the process and help you understand the mysteries of the runes.

There is much to learn about divination and rune magic. People are in need of insight and guidance. We are being asked to look to our higher selves and ascend from the mundane into a more advanced state of being. I hope this book inspires you and is a welcome part of your journey, just like writing it was for me.

RESOURCES

Books

Norse Mythology by Neil Gaiman
This is a wonderful telling of Norse mythology by one of today's greatest writers. His audiobook of this is truly inspiring.

Northern Magic: Rune Mysteries and Shamanism by Edred Thorsson
Thorsson has great insight on runework and runic magic.

Northern Mysteries & Magick by Freya Aswynn
Beautifully written, this book includes insight from a leader in the runic community. Fantastic layouts and magic make this a must-have.

The Poetic Edda: Stories of the Norse Gods and Heroes translated and edited and with an introduction by Jackson Crawford
Crawford's standard translation makes the *Poetic Edda* easy to read and understand.

A Practical Guide to The Runes by Lisa Peschel
This was one of the first rune books I purchased and has great information and descriptions.

The Prose Edda by Snorri Sturluson
This is a great resource for Northern mythology and a fantastic historical text.

Runes for Beginners by Lisa Chamberlain
This book has illuminating descriptions along with helpful correlation charts.

Taking Up the Runes: A Complete Guide to Using Runes in Spells, Rituals, Divination, and Magic by Diana L. Paxson
This is a tome of a book that offers outstanding rituals and runic ceremonies.

Online Resources

Arith Harger YouTube Channel
Arith is an inspiration for me and, as an archaeologist, offers historical insight on Northern culture. He dispels modern misconceptions and provides accurate information for any rune-worker.

Jackson Crawford YouTube Channel
Crawford offers outstanding insight on the language, runes, and culture of the Northern people throughout history.

The Rune Ways Podcast
This is my own podcast on runework and runic magic.

RuneWays.com
This is my website with helpful tips and resources for rune-workers.

REFERENCES

Aswynn, Freya. *Northern Mysteries & Magick: Runes, Gods, and Feminine Powers*, 2nd ed. St. Paul, MN: Llewellyn, 2002.

————. *Power and Principles of the Runes*. Leicestershire, England: Thoth Publications, 2008.

Blum, Ralph. *The Book of Runes: A Handbook for the Use of an Ancient Oracle*. New York: St. Martin's Press, 1984.

Chamberlain, Lisa. *Runes for Beginners*. Chamberlain Publications, 2018.

Crawford, Jackson. "The Afterlife and Hel in Norse Myth." Video, youtube.com/watch?v=VMTEFza9U5s, accessed July 2022.

————. "Poetic Edda vs. Prose Edda: The Difference" Video, youtube.com/watch?v=Z_B6NlWTy28, accessed July 2022.

————. "The Vanir." Video, youtube.com/watch?v=HFiILvbKMZM, accessed June 2022.

Farnell, Kim. *Runes Plain & Simple*. Newburyport, MA: Hampton Roads Publishing, 2016.

Gods and Monsters. "Odin's Sacrifice: Norse Mythology: Episode 4." Video, accessed July 2022.

Harger, Arith. "The First Runic Alphabet." Video, youtube.com/watch?v=ZDaDRVZeFOE, accessed June 2022.

————. "How Did Odin Become the Alfather?" Video, youtube.com/watch?v=tY_tGIrhrik, accessed June 2022.

————. "The Runes - Common Misconceptions." Video, youtube.com/watch?v=kilnLxLdCfQ, accessed June 2022.

Olsen, Kaedrich. *Runes For Transformation: Using Ancient Symbols to Change Your Life*. Newburyport, MA: Weiser Books, 2008.

Peschel, Lisa. *A Practical Guide to the Runes: Their Uses in Divination and Magick*. Woodbury, MN: Llewellyn, 1989.

Simonds, Josh. *The Beginner's Guide to Runes: Divination and Magic with the Elder Futhark Runes*. Oakland, CA: Rockridge Press, 2020.

Thorsson, Edred. *Futhark: A Handbook of Rune Magic*. Boston: Weiser Books, 2012.

RUNE INDEX

INDEX

Acknowledgments

Thanks to the following people for their support and contributions to this journey: Laurie Brekke, the fine folks at Rockridge Press, Charlie and Cindy Odorizzi and all the Next Millennium Retail Witches, Pappa Newt, Laura Ekleberry, Tracy Kyler, Kelli Miller, DreAnna Hadash, Valerie Summers, Theresa Falk, Arith Harger, and Larry Dunn.

About the Author

Wayne Brekke is a practicing rune reader, author, and clinician living in Omaha, Nebraska. He is the host of the *Rune Ways* podcast and YouTube channel as well as a working artist, musician, and business owner.

As an experienced rune weaver, Brekke seeks to help others through rune readings and spiritual consultation. His work incorporates runes, crystals, herbs, and a variety of magical practices to bring insight to his clients. Wayne is also a husband, father, and grandfather, as well as caretaker to three cats.